KEYS TO NAVIGATING THROUGH COMMON RELATIONSHIP CHALLENGES

TYRUS J. HINTON

Copyright © 2020 Tyrus J. Hinton

ISBN: 978-0-9987700-2-4 (Paperback)

Raleigh, NC

All rights reserved.
No part of this book may be reproduced or used in any manner without the written permission of the copyright owner except for the use of quotations in a book review.

Cover Designer:
Freshdesignz: Demarcus Williams

Layout Designer:
Inkcept Studio

Startwrite Publish Book Management Team:

Editors:
G.c. Simmons/Jennifer Eiland/Erin Almond

Project Manager:
Rainah Davis

Interior Book Art:
Brittany Oliver Annis

ENDORSEMENTS

No relationship avoids crisis forever, but please never forget that "crisis doesn't have to mean chaos!" This book is about to shift your perspective, your relationship, and your life.

—Marcus Gill—
Author and CEO of Marcus Gill International INC.

Whether engaged, newlywed, or veteran, Couples in Crisis will serve as an invaluable resource. I highly recommend that you add this book to your library, it is truly a powerful tool you cannot afford not to own.

— J. Michael Foster—
Author and CEO, Outrageous Living

Many couples experience seasons where one or both of the individuals contemplate whether to end their relationship or continue it. Wise individuals take this period very seriously. They do not ignore the alarms that go off when their union is plagued with negativity and issues. Couples in crisis is a powerful tool that can help you and your significant overcome difficulty, reconnect, and experience joy with one another, previously unattainable.

—Rainah M. Davis—
Author, Entrepreneur, and Vision Strategist

CONTENTS

Endorsements 3
Introduction 9
Chapter 1 **Focus** 11
    The 80/20 Rule 13
    Focus Determines Emotion 14

Chapter 2 **Foundations** 19
    Us Against the World 20
    Lesson 1: Submission 22
    Knowing Your Role 23
    Redefining Family 27

Chapter 3 **Growing Pains** 37
    The Infant Stage 39
    The Adolescent Stage 41
    The Mature Stage 46

Chapter 4 **Grown Folk Problems** 55
    Love 55
    Warning!!!! 57
    Dealing with Change 60

Chapter 5 **Money Talk** 67
    Upper, Middle, and Lower Class 68
    The Second Leading Cause for
    Divorce in America 73
    Financial Security Agreement 76
    Starting The Money Talk 80

Chapter 6 **Is it worth it?** 89
    Marriage Crisis 89
    The Terminal Illness Crisis 90

	The Affair Crisis	94
	The "Growing Apart" Crisis	95
	The Abuse Crisis	96
	Solutions	98
	Emergency Crisis Procedures for Your Marriage	100
Chapter 7	**Have I Met Everyone?**	109
	Age Difference (10 Years or More)	111
	Interracial & Intercultural Partnerships	112
	Intercultural Partnerships	113
	Same-Sex Partnerships	114
Chapter 8	**Relationship Frustration**	117
	- Options	
	- Toxic Relationships	
	- Strained Communication	
	- The Show	
Chapter 9	**Bedroom Guests**	125
	- Pornography	
	- Sex Toys	
	- Additional Partners	
Chapter 10	**Partner Political Views**	129
	- Necessary Questions	
	- Personal Views	
	- Respect	
Chapter 11	**Avoid O.P.P.**	133
	- Dysfunctional Romance	
	- Unhealthy Relationships	
	- Common Affairs	
	- Recovery Tips	

CRISIS:

A TIME OF INTENSE DIFFICULTY, TROUBLE, OR DANGER.

THE CHINESE SYMBOL FOR "CRISIS" IS A COMBINATION OF THE SYMBOL FOR DANGER AND THE SYMBOL FOR OPPORTUNITY.

INTRODUCTION

Over the last fifteen years, I've had the privilege of providing guidance to hundreds of amazing individuals and couples. Some were seriously dating and seeking marriage, some were trying to determine if they wanted this life-long commitment called marriage, some were in the process of divorce, having a change of heart and needing a mediator regarding reconciliation; and some were simply separating and wanted someone to come alongside them during this time to provide support or advice. I have also counseled couples who were trying to figure out how to strengthen their commitment to one another due to common external crises which were causing unfamiliar challenges in their relationships.

So I come to you, not only as an author penning a book, but also as a husband who has been married for over twenty-five years without interruption or separation. Prior to our marriage, we were in a committed relationship to one another for four years. We dated our last three years of high school and the first year of college and then decided to make our relationship a commitment forever. Therefore, I know a thing or two about surviving crises!

We have had to work through every crisis that you will see in the pages to come. The fortunate part for you is that I am providing you a resource so that when these relationship crises pop up in your life, you will have a roadmap to help you to navigate your way through and continue building a relationship that can and will last forever.

Additionally, I have assisted numerous individuals in walking through each type of crisis that I will mention in this book. Now some examples will be very specific while others will be more general.

Still, after sharing them all, each reader will have the answers to some challenging questions that they might find uncomfortable asking friends, family counselors, religious groups that they might be affiliated with, or one another.

If we are honest, we will admit that most people get into a relationship because they want to be happy. They get married with the goal of enhancing their own life in some way and desire that the other person will be happy with them as well. However, what's also true is that nearly no one enters a relationship with plans to experience financial challenges, family challenges, kids gone wild, infidelity, terminal diagnoses, tragic accidents, or even death. Sadly, sometimes these events find their way into our relationships. For the most part, many of us experience fairly good relationships. We usually enjoy great moments with our significant others and are happy with the lives that we are building together, but when a major crisis is thrown into the mix, the relationship typically will not survive without some type of guidance.

My hope is that after finishing this book, not only will you be able to find personal answers, but that you will also become a resource for close family, friends, business associates, partners, co- workers, and couples you may encounter —especially those caught in crisis.

危机

Chapter 1

FOCUS

In nearly all of my sessions, I open with the simple exercise of both parties writing down their ten favorite things and their ten least favorite things about one another. The purpose of this exercise is for couples to define the highest value each presents to one another, as well as the small items that could potentially cause problems for them in the future.

Will you do this exercise with me? If your answer is "Yes," take out a pen and paper right now. On the left side of the page, write down all of the special attributes of your partner (I really want you to come up with at least fifteen). Next, on the right side of the page, I want you to write down some things that bother you about your partner. What do you notice about the two lists? Is one longer than the other? Was one easier to write than the other? How do you feel about your spouse/partner right now? Do you feel more excited and in love, or do you feel irritated and ready to question the relationship?

Whenever I counsel a couple that is preparing for marriage, I always start them off with this statement: "For the next six weeks, I am going to do everything I can in these sessions to break y'all up." Once the couple gets over the initial shock of the statement, I go on to explain: "If some random dude sitting at a table asking you questions can destroy your relationship, your marriage doesn't have a chance surviving in the real world." Make sense?

In my experience, I have discovered that when most couples do this exercise, they can barely find things that they dislike about each other. Yet it brings them so much joy when they begin to think about the things that they love about each other. Interestingly enough, typically, the couple is sitting in my office because their current crisis has them reflecting on the negative instead of the positive. The purpose of this exercise is to get the couple to try something different. It's an attempt to get them to change their focus. I want to help them rewire their brain so that they can celebrate the things that they love about their mate rather than focusing on the things that they hate. Here is a major key: Believe it or not, *focus* is the key to having a happy and successful marriage.

Focus is the Key

The truth is that there are very few areas in our lives with which we are completely satisfied.

Whether it's our weight, our income level, our career status, our level of financial debt, or our overall happiness, most of us have multiple areas in our lives that are far from perfect. When it comes to our standards for our marriages/relationships, somehow this knowledge goes out of the window. We expect our relationships and our partners to be perfect, and any area of our relationship that is not exactly as we want it to be causes us immeasurable emotional pain and suffering. Again, it bears repeating that our romantic relationships are the ONLY things in our lives that we hold to this standard of perfection. Our spouse could be doing hundreds of things right, but we still choose to focus on the one thing that they are doing wrong at the moment. Thus, the 80/20 rule is real!

THE 80/20 RULE

Although your partner/spouse can be doing 80% of things right and 20% of things wrong, your mind will focus on the 20% that they are doing wrong. That small percentage can become, in your mind, a splinter that nags you to the point that you finally come to the conclusion that the only solution is divorce! And most people will leave the person who has the 80% for the person who has the 20%, only to discover that the 80% was far more important! Consequently, they wind up missing the 80%!

This is how I address this with couples:

Therapist: "There are several aspects of your life that you are unhappy with, right?"

Client: "Yes."

Therapist: "But you're not going to divorce yourself, are you? You're not going to commit suicide, right?"

Client: "No."

(Typically the answer is No. Obviously, if the client is contemplating suicide, then this has ceased to be a marital counseling session. Instead, this matter should be referred to a clinical health professional. But for the purposes of this illustration, we will continue as if they responded with a "No.")

Therapist: "How is it that you can live with the tension of the multiple areas in your life —that is, areas in which you are not happy with yourself —but you are finding it difficult to accept the one or two areas in your life where you are not happy with your spouse?

How is it that you find such grace and understanding for your flaws but seem to find your partner's flaws as complete and unacceptable deal breakers?"

At this point, I bring up the concept of focus because our emotional state is determined by what we choose to focus on. This concept is actually good news. Since we cannot control what happens to us, but we CAN control our emotional response to what happens, that puts us in the driver's seat in matters of maintaining our happiness!

FOCUS DETERMINES EMOTION

For example, if you walked out of the grocery store and discovered that you were the victim of a hit-and-run on your car, how would you feel? If someone smashed into the back of your car and caused thousands of dollars' worth of damage and THEN committed the second crime of fleeing the scene, leaving you responsible to pay for the damage, how would you *feel*?

Even though I can't hear your response, I'm sure that you wouldn't feel joyful. You would probably feel angry, sad, and victimized, right? But I want to hit you with this truth: The accident did not make you feel that way. You made a *decision* to allow yourself to feel that way because of what you chose to focus on.

Does this reaction sound a little far-fetched? Let me prove it to you. Let's alter the example to prove the point. Imagine that you walk out of the same grocery store and find the same hit-and-run damage to your car. Only this time I want you to imagine that you are a part of a special government program that is going to pay you ONE MILLION DOLLARS every time you're the victim of a hit-and-run.

NOW, how do you feel? Are you still feeling sad? Are you still feeling like a victim? Of course not! You're HAPPY that someone hit your vehicle! Instead of feeling helpless because you can't stop a hit-and-run from happening again, you are HOPEFUL that it will happen again!

What is my point here? My point is that in both of the examples the same event happened. The only difference between your feeling sad and your feeling excited is the decision that you made about what to focus on. That decision, and that decision alone, determined how you would feel. The good news is that at any given time, you have access to joy or sadness, depression or hope, stress or peace. You have the power to make the decision about what you will focus on, and that decision will determine how you feel! Can you imagine how many relationship problems could be avoided if people just took ownership of what they focused on?

Focus is the key to the success or failure of your marriage/relationship, especially when you and your spouse/partner are trying to successfully navigate through a crisis.

Did you read the fine print?

Believe it or not, your wedding vows prepared you and your spouse for most of the crisis areas that you all would face throughout your marriage. The "fine print" in those vows was designed to shape our focus ahead of time so that when the issues arose, we already had a pre-determined focus and response to them.

Think about it: we are supposed to love "for better or worse, in sickness or in health, poverty or wealth, 'til death, do us part." Everything that could ever attack your marriage is covered in these sacred vows. But as always, "the devil is in the details."

What I mean by "the devil is in the details" is simply this: The marriage vows may cover the general idea of what you should focus on in marriage, but they don't deal with specifics. In the "sickness" part, the vows never explicitly mention the different types of sicknesses that might come up. It's one thing to deal with a headache or the common cold, but what about a cancer diagnosis or loss of sight or vision? What about the loss of limbs due to an accident or diabetes?

I once counseled a couple whose husband was cheating on his wife. When I asked why he was cheating, the husband said, "Because chemo has dried her out, and she can't have sex anymore." This response was not typically the type of thing that readily comes to mind when you think of loving someone in "sickness" and in "health," is it? But don't worry, ladies, I am not leaving you out. I know of a marriage in which the wife was cheating on her significantly older husband. What was the reason of the infidelity? You guessed it ╳erectile dysfunction. A lifetime of eating greasy, fatty foods led to his inability to have or sustain an erection. And if you talked to the wife, she felt *justified* in her cheating because her husband was not able to "take care of her" as he's "supposed to."

But wait, there's more! What if the sickness is mental? Do you realize how many couples are suffering with this ailment and/or contemplating divorce because one or both spouses are suffering from undiagnosed mental illness? Do you know what clinical depression does to your overall mood?

Do you know what it does to your sex life? Your spending habits? Your cleaning habits?

Can you imagine trying to get along with a person who is exhibiting these negative traits and thinks that his or her behavior is normal? Can you imagine the effect the behavior can have on a couple's intimacy when one spouse is perpetually "not in the mood?" What about manic/depression (bi-polar), paranoia, schizophrenia, oppositional defiant disorder, etc.? Every one of these mental challenges can:

- Sabotage intimacy,
- Poison familial interactions,
- Affect financial decisions,
- Keep someone from being able to become employed or *remain* employed, and can
- Negatively impact communication to the point at which the husband and wife are always arguing and can never seem to pinpoint the reason why.

Chances are that you never imagined that mental health or poor dietary habits could be the "sicknesses" that threaten to destroy your marriage, but statistics confirm that they can be.

Are you *focused* yet? If you are not, become so, because these challenges are serious.

Your wedding vows do the best that they can to prepare you for the difficult journey ahead but unfortunately, the vows do not explain the different types of situations that might take place or the different kinds of tragedies that might occur. I ran across an article by Web MD that conveyed this chilling report:

"Studies show that marriages in which one spouse has a chronic illness are more likely to fail if the spouses are young.

And spouses who are caregivers are six times more likely to be depressed than spouses who do not need to be caregivers." Wow. Just wow!

"Even in the best marriages, it's hard. You feel trapped, out of control, and helpless", says clinical psychologist Rosalind Kalb, Vice President of the Professional Resource Center at the National Multiple Sclerosis Society.

But even with all of these challenges, there is hope. I am here to bring/give you hope.

危机

Chapter 2

FOUNDATIONS

Allow me to open with this question: How solid is the foundation on which your relationship is built?

I realize that I am kind of dating myself here, but consider the song which asked the above question in a different way in the 1988 hit from the group New Edition. It says:

> *Sunny days, everybody loves them, tell me, baby,*
> *"Can you stand the rain?" (Can you stand it?) Storms will come (I know, I know all the days won't be perfect)*
> *This we know for sure (But tell me can you stand it)*
> *"Can you stand the rain?" (Can you stand the rain?)*
> *Songwriters: James Harris / James Samuel Harris / Terry Lewis*
> *Can You Stand the Rain lyrics © Kobalt Music Publishing Ltd.*

This song's refrain is my question to every couple...can your relationship stand the rain, storms, and hurricanes of life? If your answer is "No," or if you are not sure, that uncertainty is okay. (Honesty is always okay. Lying to your spouse or to yourself is a point at which things get interesting...)

One of the first declarations you will need to make is this: "It is my partner and me against the world!"

What that means is that you must decide that nothing or anyone can or will come between you and your spouse, love-of-your-life, knight-in- shining armor, sweet thing —whatever you may call him or her.

US AGAINST THE WORLD

My wife and I decided over thirty years ago prior to marriage that it was going to be "us against the world!" NOTHING and NO ONE is more important than protecting the bond of your love. Now, I am not suggesting that you remain in a relationship in which there is anything immoral, unethical, illegal, or abusive occurring, but what I am suggesting is that you do not allow life, money, careers, kids, in-laws/out-laws —or just little crazy stuff to cause you two to drift apart. In fact, it is important that you share dreams and plans so that you two can remain in agreement.

A Matter of Life and Death

On July 17, 1981, two suspended walkways through the lobby of the Hyatt Regency in Kansas City, Missouri collapsed, killing 114 and injuring 200 people at a tea dance. The collapse was due to a late change in design which altered the method in which the rods supporting the walkways were connected to them, and at the same time inadvertently doubled the forces on the connection. The failure highlighted the need for good communication between design engineers and contractors and rigorous checks on designs, especially on contractor-proposed design changes. The failure is a standard case study in engineering courses around the world, and this study is used to teach the importance of ethics in engineering.

Just as in the construction example listed above, if we do not carefully construct our relationships/ marriages on solid foundations with proper materials and lots of communication, we too will undoubtedly experience irreparable damage to our hearts and lives. Building your relationship on the right foundation is literally a matter of life and death. In practically every aspect of my ministry, I am constantly reminded that relationships are the one thing that we commit to forever without any real training. Instead, we tend to base our relationships on what we have observed whether it be from our family or close friends.

But the same way that the tragedy above provides a case study for engineering students so that they know how to construct buildings correctly, we also need to gain some education, knowledge, and understanding about relationships in order to build relationships on firm foundations of concrete and not of sand.

For example, if your spouse started experiencing chest pains, you wouldn't attempt to do open heart surgery on him or her because you're not a trained doctor. If your car's "service engine soon" light came on, you wouldn't pop open the hood and commence to take the engine apart to find the issue because you're not a trained mechanic. If someone sued you for ten million dollars, you wouldn't try to represent yourself because you're not trained in the art and practice of jurisprudence.

The interesting piece is that even though we know that each of the problem areas listed above require professionals who have had *years* of training and years of experience in their respective areas, when it comes to the area of relationships, we somehow consider ourselves qualified to "operate" on the dysfunction in our relationship. We consider ourselves qualified to diagnose and dissect the problems that arise and subsequently provide a viable solution. Even though we know that people attend school for years to become professional marriage counselors, we still think that we can do their jobs as well as they can do them after many years of training with no training "under our belts."

Let's make this decision right now: The foundation of my relationship will be built on the solid foundation of training, communication, and love!

LESSON 1: SUBMISSION

Submission has become a dirty word in our society, but it should not be. You must commit or re-commit to your partner/spouse's being the most important person in the world to you. Under all circumstances, you must be willing to submit to *one another*—no matter how difficult doing so may be.

In the book *Rocking the Roles: Building a Win-Win Marriage*, authors Lewis and Hendricks describe submission this way:

"...any teacher who says wives should be submissive to their husbands is liable to set off a firestorm of controversy. Yet even the Bible uses the term. Furthermore, submission is presented in almost every biblical example as an act of honor."

While most people present this topic from a one-sided perspective (the wife should submit to her husband), the Bible does not. Ephesians 5:22 says, "Wives, submit yourselves to your own husbands." But the verse immediately before it says that we are to submit ourselves to *one another* in the fear of God. In other words, in a healthy and functional relationship, BOTH parties do their share of submitting. This principle applies to everyone —faith-based or not.

Think of it this way: No one expects you to outright defy an assignment from your boss, manager, or team leader. That person has the authority in that particular situation, and you are expected to subjugate your opinions and thoughts and to comply. Well, in relationships you must be ready to submit, yield, and comply to one another in specific areas. I know of some relationships in which only one person cooks because they both want to live! No, I am kidding. But think about something that your spouse does significantly better than you. It does not matter whether it is traditionally a "male" or "female" role, it just makes sense to let the person who is more capable in that area take charge.

KNOWING YOUR ROLE

I know couples who have interchangeable roles. They iron the clothes, prepare meals, and/or keep the home, just to name a few, because that "chore" is their strength and "place" of agreement.

Traditionally, specific genders did certain things. Women cooked, cleaned, took care of the children, and generally dealt with the issues of the home. In contrast, men traditionally were the bread winners. They went out into the workforce and provided the financial stability for the household. In addition, men did the manual labor jobs around the house: cutting the grass, taking out the trash, washing the cars, and fixing things around the house.

We live in a new era now, and if you want your relationship to be successful, it will be necessary for the two of you to have honest conversations about each of these areas and then agree on what's best for your relationship. I know of a couple whose wife's father was a chef, so she grew up watching a man do all of the cooking. Perhaps you may know of a relationship in which the husband is much more particular about having a clean house than the wife is; therefore, he is usually the one to clean it up. Problems arise when you have a man who is adamant about having a clean house but refuses to clean it because that is a "woman's job." A good rule of thumb is, "If it bothers you, fix it!" If the dirty dishes bother you, wash them. If the bed not being made bothers you, then make it. If the kids' homework is not being done to your satisfaction, then YOU help them with their homework. Again, problems arise when YOU have the high standards but you want to make the "bone of contention" someone else's responsibility to keep up with the duties of that standard.

If one spouse is clearly better at handling money than the other, then that spouse should be in charge of the money. Just because the husband is the head of the house doesn't mean that he should be in charge of handling the money. A huge part of good leadership is knowing how to delegate. A good way to model mutual submission is for the man to submit to his wife when she says, "This is an unnecessary purchase and it doesn't fit into the overall vision that we have set for our family at this time." The bottom line is that it is important make a decision that you are going to protect each other and submit to one another in love. If you submit, you, my friends, are starting out with a good foundation.

I know this declaration to be true because, again, I have been married to same woman without separation for over twenty-five years. Don't get me wrong, it was extremely challenging for us in the beginning and we had many bumps in the road along the way. Let me share a portion of our story.

Our Story

I was quite young when I started dating my wife. In fact, we were both high school students and attended two separate schools. Back in the day, the older generations used to call it "puppy love." My mom repeatedly told me that I had no clue what love was! She often reminded me that my real focus should be on my studies, and not to worry because I would know when the right one came along. Now, to be clear, it is not that my mom didn't care for my girlfriend, my mom was just was concerned that something unforeseen would divert my attention from my schoolwork since I often struggled with maintaining above-average grades.

Reminiscing, I distinctly recall how different our families were. Her mom was very spiritual, private, quiet, structured, routine, and stern in countenance demeanor. She didn't play any games. I believed that I had made a major breakthrough when she began to like me. Her mom realized I was a religious, respectable, well-mannered, neatly dressed young man who treated her daughter with respect. She welcomed me to visit her home (with her present, of course) as often as I liked after school and on the weekends. However, behind all of that goodness remained our biggest difference: my girlfriend (her daughter) was an honors student who was very disciplined in her studies, and I was her polar opposite.

My mom was similar: quiet, spiritual, structured, routine, and neither was she to be played with. My mom often said, "You play with toys, not with me!" While our mothers had the same core values, they were expressed very differently in our families. My family constantly hosted big family gatherings. We were loud and were over the top with everything. Every time we came together, it was like a holiday of some sort. There were always multiple conversations taking place at the same time, thus causing the noise level to remain at an all-time high. We had a wide assortment of revelers: aunts; uncles; sisters; brothers; cousins; play cousins; neighborhood friends; family members; co-workers; church members; and sometimes *their* friends and family. Our house would get packed very quickly. Now my girlfriend's side was very private and quiet. I never found there to be a crowded or loud home. Few in number—always they knew name-by-name everyone who was in the home at all times.

Additionally, my girlfriend was raised by her mother, while I was raised by my paternal grandmother. This difference resulted in our upbringings, varying largely in both age and views.

Talk about a challenge.

Fast forwarding in the story, we dated during our last three years of high school and during our freshman year of college. Around this time of schooling, we experienced our first family crisis. My family began to have an issue with the amount of time, energy, and effort that I was putting into my relationship. My family started to put pressure on me to spend more time with them. They really became upset when I chose to be with my girlfriend rather than attend a family gathering. This decision sent my girlfriend and me spiraling directly toward "family crisis" mode (Family crisis is often the silent killer of any relationship! The Bible says, "For this cause shall a man leave his father and mother and cleave to his wife, and the two shall become one flesh." In order for any marriage to work, your spouse has to be the most important person in your life. ALL familial relationships must be secondary and treated as such.).

At this point, I had to determine whether or not I would defend my girlfriend and our relationship or allow my family to treat me as if she didn't matter and as if I were still everyone's favorite little boy (I really was the "Golden Child"). However, I learned a very valuable lesson during that period of my life. The lesson is that anytime the family interferes with your relationship, a crisis is inevitable.

Crisis is defined as a time of intense difficulty, trouble, or danger.

REDEFINING FAMILY

Our relationship began to experience some very intense difficulty because of my inability to defend our relationship to my family with the confidence needed to match or outmatch their interference. Based on my family's history of bad romantic relationships, we had a very negative, selfish view and approach to having any type of relationship with someone outside of the home. As far as my family was concerned, the other person is **temporary**, but we are your family **forever**.

While being considered temporary is true in some respects, when building relationships, we cannot afford to see the person we are building with as temporary. When our view of the person we are with is long-term, we then are able to defend our decision with confidence and clarity. Now, I am not suggesting that you ignore the warning signs from abuse and the such, I am only referring to a relationship that is otherwise a healthy one.

Looking back at my childhood, I realize that my family did an amazing job at preparing me for college, careers, and financial success, but there was almost an inability to truly let the eagle out of the nest and fly when it came to relationships. It was as if my family never imagined or considered that at some point I would "leave and cleave" to my wife. At that time, they couldn't see her as a wife, she was just my girlfriend. I had to remind my family that they prepared me for life and love in the future. I honestly do not think that they disagreed with me in theory. The truth was that they just hadn't set a realistic timeframe for when I would come into my manhood or what my manhood would mean for to/in their future.

So in selfishness, they began to make statements and to plant negative seeds that would cause me to look at my girlfriend differently, and this tactic worked for a point. Sometimes, though ever so slightly, I changed my perspective a little. It's not that I was weak minded; it was just that up until that point in my life, my family's voices were the ones that resonated with me the most, because I had been listening to them about every major decision that I had ever made in my entire life.

The situation began to get worse as my actions and words became different, and the strain that it placed on my relationship with my girlfriend was almost unbearable. My girlfriend and I went days without speaking (which is very unhealthy when you are building a relationship) all because of my family and confusion. The truth is that selfishness will never work when you are trying to build a relationship.

Thank goodness, my girlfriend and I had a few seasoned couples around us who had been married for a few years and provided some valuable insight about what was happening with us. Fortunately, they provided the intervention we needed to begin to put our relationship back on the right track.

Many times our families struggle with letting go. Remember, I was the golden child. As the relationship evolves, it should be your mission to believe in your choice so much that you are prepared to do a 30-second commercial confirming your relationship's strength at any time. We must always be ready to defend what we believe in, and this should be even more the case with your developing relationship. I cannot stress enough, my conviction is that if you believe in your relationship, then you must be prepared to defend it. Many times, you will have to defend your relationship to your family, first. They have to see and trust that you are convinced that this is the best possible decision for you at that time.

Try this really quickly. Do a 30-second commercial about the one that you are in a relationship with right now. Talk about all of his or her amazing qualities and why you love being with him or her. Now think- was that easy? Or was it more challenging than you thought? Are you really convinced of the strength of your relationship?

If you have previously made bad relationship choices, often family members will keep bringing up your past relationship(s). Well, that's great, now you can use your past poor relationships as leverage to support your decision even more. Compliment the differences of your new choice, and be ready to share all of the great moments that you and your new partner experience. Share the way you overcome and work through challenges to remain a solid couple.

Here are a few questions that you may have to ask yourself as you determine if you are dealing with a family crisis:

- Is my family too involved? What would my family's over-involvement look like if they were?
- Does my family respect my decision/mate? What words/actions have they shown to prove that they respect and support my decision to be with this person?
- Is my mate uncomfortable with or around my family? What traits would he or she exhibit if he or she were comfortable/uncomfortable?

Take your time and answer these questions honestly. If you find your answers to any of these questions troubling, we might just need to get you out of crisis!

Is my family too involved?

Think about your relationship as a private bank account. We will call it a "relationship" account. Who controls the deposits and withdrawals? When you begin to see things changing and suspect suspicious activity, do you make change immediately to avoid further inconvenience?

You must be intentional about not allowing unauthorized withdrawals from your relationship account. I suggest that you accept only positive deposits in this account which cause growth by agreement between the two of you. You wouldn't allow people to make withdrawals from your bank account without your permission, right? In the same way, you shouldn't allow ANYONE (family, friends, etc.) to say or do anything that takes away from the value of your relationship in the eyes of you or your spouse.

Since my family was very close and greatly involved, I one day made the decision to move out pretty abruptly. I realized that if I didn't move out at that particular time, I never would. There were no pressing family issues or anything of that sort. I was just ready to practice what Mom had been preparing me for —independence. It's one thing to talk about it, but I truly needed the opportunity to *practice* what my Mom had been preparing me for all my life. My Mom laid a strong foundation of faith, values, and family. I knew how to handle myself upon leaving home. It was time to flee the nest.

Be mindful of any type of family involvement/ conversation because, unfortunately, there can always be a selfish aspect at play. In order for you to come out of crisis mode, you will have to eliminate negative family involvement and strongly defend your mate. I even suggest taking a break from both families as you learn one another. This family break increases your opportunity to learn one another without the influence of the opinions of random family members. For whatever reason, family loves to reminisce on the good "ole" days. This tendency may not be conducive for your relationship as those are past reference points which can turn ugly quickly.

I strongly urge you to spend time with the question, "What would my relationship look like if my family were too involved?" Seek the counsel of wise friends and married people. You should also ask your partner/spouse what he or she thinks about your family involvement. Sometimes we can be so used to family involvement that we don't notice the effect that it is having on us and our relationship. For the most part, we know that our family loves us and wants the best for us. But sometimes people can inadvertently sabotage our relationship thinking that they are doing us a favor.

Here are some questions to ask yourself:

- Do I feel better or worse about my relationship after talking to my family member?
- Is my opinion of my partner higher or lower after talking to my family member?
- Is my family member dealing with any pain or bitterness from a failed relationship in their own lives that may be affecting their perspective on this matter? Are they even qualified to advise me on this matter?
- Every relationship is different. Are my family members capable of separating the nuances of my relationship from the failures of theirs?

Does my family respect my decision/mate?

The only way your family knows to respect your mate is by your example. It is important that you are very clear on how much you respect what they offer you and how they elevate you. *Do you admire their intelligence, their style, their sense of business, their educational accomplishments?* If so, these are the things that you need to highlight to your family. You must be convinced that you picked a winner. Once you are convinced, they will be convinced. In many cases, once a respectful aspect is presented *to* your family, that same aspect will be repeated *by* your family.

Watch what you say! I remember talking about how intelligent my girlfriend was. I talked about her academic accomplishments. I talked about how she helped me study and even pass a few exams. I set the bar high. Good thing I graduated, or else it would've been a different story! But my family respected her intelligence because I did.

Remember that this is not the time to lie to your family or yourself. Your family has known you all of your life, and in some cases, they can know you better than you know yourself. If there are aspects or qualities about your partner that truly bother you, it will be very difficult to hide your disdain from your family. Just be honest about how you feel.

Never make the mistake of becoming a used car salesman. People despise a used car salesman because they have a habit of presenting the car's good qualities while hiding or just plain lying about the car's flaws. If the car has over 100,000 miles, tell me! If the car has been in an accident, tell me! If the car is due for some costly maintenance, tell me!

The worst thing you can do is hide flaws from me that I find out about after I'm invested. Hiding flaws creates two problems. First, you have broken my trust and now I am not sure if I can trust you or anything you say about this relationship in the future. Second, you rob me of the opportunity to make an informed decision. Perhaps I want the car and don't care that it has over 100,000 miles. Perhaps I am comfortable with the fact that it has been in an accident. Either way, lying about your partner's flaws is going to automatically create problems in your marriage, and if you don't trust the *actual* qualities of your partner to be enough for your family, then you might want to question whether or not they are the one for you.

*Consider the following:

What are you saying about your mate? Do you ever make negative comments about your mate unintentionally? Do you ever say or do things which hint or suggest that they are not consistent in their relationship with you? These comments can be an indicator as to why they are not respecting your mate.

Remember that your responsibility is to *assist* your family with respecting your choice. Your family is just looking out for you and your best interest.

Nevertheless, selfishness on the part of the family will cause them to automatically look for the flaws in your potential life partner as opposed to looking for the greatness and seeing what you see. And this seeking of potential flaws is not a bad thing. Your family is supposed to look out for you. It is likewise your job to convince them that they have nothing to worry about. It is your job to answer the questions about your spouse's character. It is your job to show the respect that you want repeated in your presence and absence.

Is my mate uncomfortable around my family?

Your mate being uncomfortable around your family is a big relationship issue. Remember how I shared with you how different our families were?

For instance, we were loud. We spoke louder than the other conversations going on nearest to us. My girlfriend was used to quiet and controlled atmospheres, to very conservative tones with one person's speaking at a time. We must bear in mind that our mate's level of comfort will depend on the information that we have shared and the energy we continue to invest into making them feel comfortable. All new environments can be scary. It is your job as the person who is used to your family environment to go out of your way to make sure that your spouse feels comfortable. As individuals, we all have the tendency to pre-judge people and situations based on the lessons that we were taught and the way that we were raised. Your mate will be only as comfortable as you allow them to be.

In my case when we were young, I told my girlfriend, "I am the golden child." I used to say, "I am the favorite." As a result, when she came around, there was an understanding that they would treat me extremely special—almost like a baby. Therefore, it was my responsibility to share the honest truth without making her feel it would be the most awkward encounter ever. The same holds true for her. She was the honors student, the family genius that everyone loved and adored. It was equally difficult for me to fit in with her family since my looks and charm could only take me so far. The bottom line is that you are the bridge to make everything smooth and comfortable for your spouse.

You also are responsible for speaking up on your mate's behalf. You never want to let your mate feel alone when they are with you and their family at the same time. You are the representative for the relationship at the family dinners, fun nights, reunions, and Sunday dinner.

We have covered a lot of material in this section. Think back to the beginning of this chapter, and review the foundation of your relationship. I want you to dig *deeper* within and ask yourself the following questions:

1. **What is our relationship built on currently? Is it built on CONCRETE OR SAND?**

    Do we have solid communication, trust, honesty and deep familial relationships so that we can give our relationship the best chance to succeed?

    If not, what steps can we take to construct a solid foundation?

If we believe that we have a solid foundation, what steps can we put in place to ensure that we do not begin to see cracks in our foundation?

2. **Have I allowed any family, friend, or otherwise to make an unauthorized withdrawal from our relationship account?**

Are there family members or friends who make negative comments about my partner, comments that make me look at my partner differently or lessen my opinion of him or her?

If so, what am I doing to address that? If I discovered that someone was making unauthorized withdrawals from my actual bank account, I would take immediate action to stop that from happening and I would try my best to restore the money that was taken from the account. Am I being just as vigilant about protecting the value of my relationship?

Chapter 3

GROWING PAINS

Every stage of human development comes with its own set of painful challenges and adjustments. Infants have to adjust to life on the "outside."

Toddlers have to learn language, numbers, sharing, and how to interact with other human beings. This stage is a particularly painful process for the toddler because in order to successfully navigate it, the toddler has to acknowledge the fact that he or she is not the center of the universe as he or she had previously been as an infant. Some adults have still not successfully navigated this developmental stage and still throw temper tantrums when they don't get their way or receive the special attention that they think they deserve.

Adolescence is arguably the hardest stage developmentally because the adolescent is stuck between two worlds: childhood and adulthood.

He or she is simultaneously too old to be a child and too young to be an adult. He or she is asked to relinquish the comforts of childhood without being able to experience the joys and freedom of making adult decisions. This is a painful stage and again, many adults fail to navigate this stage successfully. Consequently, his or her interpersonal relationships suffer because he or she never finished fully developing, and for this reason are not sure how to interact with others in healthy ways.

Just as in the stages of human development, relationships have to grow as well. A relationship goes through an infancy stage, toddler stage, adolescent stage, and finally an adult stage. The process of growing from infancy to adulthood is painful, no matter what arena it's in. One of the biggest challenges that people in relationships face is that they expect a relationship that has just started to exhibit all of the characteristics of a fully matured relationship.

The Empty Box

Starting a relationship is like having an empty box. When you first start the relationship, there is nothing in the box. If you want there to be trust, love, joy, teamwork, and commitment in the box, then you have to put them there. Hear me clearly: They are not *automatically* there. So many people break up or get divorced because they expected "fully matured" trust and commitment in a relationship that had just started. But in the same way that you wouldn't expect a newborn baby to graduate from college and buy a home, you shouldn't expect a "newborn" relationship to be able to handle "adult" challenges.

Trust must be earned. It is not just handed out, no matter what people say. Commitment must be developed over time. There is no such thing as having a rock-solid commitment from day one just because you call someone your boyfriend or girlfriend. Relationships today are struggling today because people are assuming that they have had a mature relationship from the beginning. Thus, when the immature relationship inevitably reveals the signs of immaturity, the person in the relationship immediately gives up hope in the relationship.

Did you ever think that you would be having these crazy conversations about relationships? It's supposed to be easy, right? We're just supposed to meet someone, fall in love, and live happily ever after, right?

Wrong.

Oh so very, VERY wrong.

A popular television commercial says, "Life comes at you fast." This statement is especially true for relationships. There is no such thing as "Happily Ever After." There is only the hard work that leads to the painful process of growth.

THE INFANT STAGE

Our first three children were all eleven months apart. Yes, you read it correctly, eleven months apart. We thought that the diaper changing phase would *never* end. We had babies for three years straight and depended on information from our parents about the best practices for everything.

Remember that in the previous chapter I pointed out how different our families are. So while one side thought it was best to let the babies open up their lungs by crying, the other side was convinced that we should avoid letting them cry —period. While we did use some of the best practices from both sides, we also had some external influences which assisted us with establishing agreements of our own for our little family.

The early years were trying. We worked opposite shifts for a little while to save daycare costs. I worked nights, and my wife worked part-time in the day. Looking back, I realized that this period was the infancy stage of our marriage in more ways than one. It was during this time that we learned our "love languages" and how to "walk" through the challenges of our marriage. I remember picking up a second job to ensure that we had more than enough for our family. I worked second jobs a few times in the earlier years of our marriage. We committed to making the relationship work by working together.

We had a few endured times of crises during the infant stages:

- THREE DAYS of labor with our daughter,
- Fetal distress with our second son, and then
- AML (Acute Myloid Leukemia) with the baby boy at that time.

Talk about a couple in crisis!

We found ourselves in crisis mode with our children at every turn during the infancy stage of our marriage. We confronted major decisions to make with each crisis surrounding each child. Each decision affected how we grew as a couple and how our marriage and family evolved and developed. We often reflect on the crises we encountered when we were all in the infant stage and how we handled them.

As a couple, you will invariably experience some type of crisis during the infancy stage of your relationship. It is almost impossible to avoid.

While your crisis may be totally different from ours, consider these few practical tips:

1. Make time to talk with one another.
2. Plan a weekly date night/day with just the two of you and no children.
3. Learn your spouse's love language (Quality Time, Physical Touch, Words of Affirmation, Acts of Service, Gifts).
4. Consult one another about decisions before reaching out to others (Keep the value of one another's voice high).
5. Acknowledge that you are in the infancy stage of your relationship. Don't place heavy expectations on your young relationship. Doing so is likely to bring about pressure, which your young relationship may not be equipped to handle. Just as you can ruin the development of a child by expecting too much from him or her too soon, you can also ruin the development of your new relationship by putting too much pressure on it too soon.

Also, during our infancy stage, we focused on learning how to manage our time with work, daycare, continuing education, and extra-curricular activities as a family.

In our opinion (my wife's and mine), we had matters under control and were doing well to be young, married with three children, and having very little assistance from both sides of the family. We used the time of our infancy stage to learn how to truly lean on each other. All we had was one another.

THE ADOLESCENT STAGE

Here is a quick lesson that we did *not* learn prior to each crisis listed above. This lesson falls under the heading "Roles and Responsibilities." A major issue that we had to address was the increased and shifting load of responsibilities.

Unfortunately, too many couples that I have counseled wait until tthey are in the heat of crisis to discuss roles and responsibilities within the household. Since the demands of any type of crisis alone can be difficult; if possible, try to take some time to discuss what life's routine will look like for you both. If you are already in it, then the time has come for some honest conversation(s), which leads us to the next challenge.

Communication

Communication is one of the most important sections of the entire book. It is absolutely imperative that you make a commitment to do whatever you have to do to get or keep the lines of communication open. If there is ever a time to speak the truth, it's now. Your relationship will impact everything, including the children that you both love so much.

One way that I suggest that you keep the lines of communication open is to schedule time together. Be intentional about focusing on the emotional needs of your spouse and try to understand that the needs are always evolving. It can become very easy for one party to completely shut down and focus only on themselves depending on what they have seen modeled in their homes. One party can be willing to talk through everything, while the other has to take a significant amount of time to process it all. It is critically important for both parties to work out an effective system that works for both each other.

We all know that opposites attract. Typically, one spouse is the "talker," and the other spouse is quieter and more reserved. The talkative spouse typically wants to address conflict immediately while emotions are still high. The more reserved spouse, however, tends to want to engage in a "cooling off" period in order for the couple to collect their thoughts and calm down emotionally so that they can be in an emotional-free space to have a calm and rational conversation about their feelings.

Take it from me (I learned the hard way), it is NOT a good idea to make the non-talkative spouse talk about their feelings before they are ready. This is a fool-proof recipe for a fight! And while I do not recommend putting off emotionally volatile conversations for days or weeks, it may be helpful to give your spouse up to 24 hours to collect their thoughts and feelings before attempting to have a rational conversation. Always remember that it is selfish to try to force your partner to talk just because YOU are ready to talk. A huge part of developing effective communication is learning your partner's best practices for communication and honoring them. Honoring your spouse's communication style is an act of love. If one spouse does not honor the other's communication style or tries to force them to adopt *their* style, it will lead to major problems and ultimately attack the foundation of the marriage.

Argument or FIGHT?

There is a difference between an argument and a fight.

An argument is a calm, rational discussion about an issue that the two of you disagree about. A fight is a period in which you are no longer addressing the issue and you are intentionally saying things to hurt the other person's feelings. For example: "That's why I ain't never liked yo mama." "That's why you could never satisfy me in bed." "I should have listened to my mother and stayed with my Ex." "I never should have married you!"

Words spoken in anger can never be taken back. Apologies don't change the truth of the words or the damage that they have caused. Although couples should argue, couples should never fight.

I can remember times when the kids were small and my wife and I had communication breakdowns. What is more, I had no words for what was happening in our lives because I couldn't understand the communication breakdowns. I had not seen it before; I didn't know what to say or the right way to say it. There were many times when I thought that the best idea was just to be quiet. That thought was based on what I had learned growing up. My mom would often say, "Think what you are thinking." That saying meant that if you kept your thoughts and emotions to yourself, no one could ever read your thoughts or take anything you had said the wrong way. This advice was well-intentioned, and it came from a loving heart and a sincere desire to help. But it was also coming from a lady who had been broken from her relationship and had developed multiple defense mechanisms to shield her from the pain.

Well, when starting a family, we do not have the luxury of being able to go into shutdown mode and still maintain a healthy family. We have to remain open. It is important that we do the hard work of talking through the most trying parts —from diaper changing to bottle temperature to bath water temperature to sleeping times and even clothing. Because all conversations are necessary and both parties must be willing to listen without the intent to respond until given the opportunity, timing, prayer, and levelheadedness. Remember that communication happens two ways and that you must give one another the opportunity to express yourselves.

Whenever I counsel a couple, one of the first questions that I ask them is, "Are you willing to do the work?" Relationships are hard work. And though open, honest, and vulnerable conversation is one of the hardest parts of a relationship, it is absolutely necessary. I want to be clear here about the importance of doing the work of communication, for when I ask a couple if they are willing to do the hard work of communication (listening, forgiving, letting their guards down and changing the way they think and interact), if they say, "NO," then that response is officially the END of the session, and I will no longer counsel them. So, yes, it is serious.

Start by asking yourself the question, "Am I truly willing to do the work?"

Your Network Changes

We had our children so young and so close together that most, if not all of our friends didn't have any children. Our children got on everyone's nerves, but we still wanted to be with our friends. Things are different today.

People are waiting a little longer to grow their families, whether it be naturally, blending and/or adoption. In fact, most folks are not married and with children at ages twenty and twenty-one. The good part for you is that the world has become both human and (fur baby) friendly. This will be especially important for you to be aware of as your single friends and/or associates may not want to be bothered, which can cause a conflict in your home.

In addition, you and your partner/spouse need to set parameters prior to expanding your family to ensure that you avoid this crisis. If not, you will be consistently desiring a life that you once had and no longer have access to which will ultimately create another crisis. There is hope for you. Social media networking platforms of all kinds are available to aid you with changing your company and identifying the healthiest relationships for your situation.

Ultimately, married couples with children typically have greater fellowship with other married couples with children. This statement is by no means a rule or law, just more of a practical observation based upon the numerous nuances that come with being married and having children. Single, childless people don't have to deal with the same challenges that married parents do. I have numerous single, childless friends, but I am no longer available to hang out late every weekend and party like a rock-star.

As your life grows and changes, it is wise to *accept* those changes and evolve with them. Refusing to do so will create resentment. This acceptance is not only true regarding the changes that come with becoming a parent, but it also applies to the changes that come with getting married, period. There's nothing quite like the crisis of being married to someone who doesn't want to be married but refuses to make the necessary adjustments to abate this train wreck waiting to happen because of misery.

THE MATURE STAGE

Once your relationship reaches its maturity, usually the types of problems that you will deal with will change. What comes to mind first is dealing with school-aged children. As your child or children become school-aged, your relationship will be tested in new and exciting ways. For example, you may be released from the burden of an expensive daycare bill, diapers, and formula, and one spouse may be returning to work after staying home to care for the child in those early years. Statistics show that for couples with school-aged kids, the chores/responsibilities become the most combative issue. Fathers are doing more childcare today than they did in previous generations. The common consensus is that everyone is equal.

In 2018, the Institute for Family Studies reported that the most common area of contention is chores, along with responsibilities. Nearly half of couples with kindergarten-aged children (forty-nine percent) said that they argued about chores' responsibilities "often" or "sometimes." Additionally, forty-three percent had arguments about money, forty-one percent about the children, and thirty-eight percent about being too tired for sex.

Can you imagine what the numbers are TODAY?

Those are the issues that we must get on one accord about as quickly as possible because at this age, couples still have authority over the children, but in the next phase, couples begin to lose a little authority and drift into more of an influence-capacity the older their children get.

Your Teens/Screenagers: GEN Y/Z (iGen)-

My wife and I often fist bump one another by way of celebrating the survival of the teenage years. If you are not careful, the teenage years will drive the biggest distance between you and your spouse/partner.

We remember the teenagers telling each of us two totally different stories. The next thing my wife and knew, we would be having an intense conversation and even arguing about a decision that one of us had made without consulting the other. It's crazy how that works.

Miscommunication throws you straight into crisis mode. If your teenager(s) is (are) perfect, then you can skip over to the next chapter. In our limited experience of raising three teenagers, we can tell you that crisis can hit the couple during the teenage phase. A good rule of thumb in these "teenage situations" is not to make a decision without consulting your partner first, especially if you know that you and your spouse have drastically different views on parenting. It is absolutely imperative that you as the parents present a united front regarding the children. Failure to do so will result in chaos.

Digital Natives

For most adults, phones are a communication device and/or a means to conduct business transactions, but they are not our sole means of relational interaction. However, many of us were born in times before the internet, mobile devices, apps, video calling, or online video streaming services existed.

Generations Y and Z are the first generations to be born in the age of digital technology, thus labeling them "digital natives" seems appropriate.

As a result, their phones are an extension of themselves. And social media is a critical part of how they communicate. Social media is important for parents to note because modern parents have a tendency to "over-parent" in ways where the parents need to show grace and "under-parent" in ways where they need to pay more attention. This is certainly the case in the digital age. The same way we noted that communication was important for you as the couple, it is critical that one or both parents is able to communicate clearly and openly with the teen. We are living in a time when children will share their feelings on social media with their "friends" before they will share them with the actual family in whose house they are living. This trend is dangerous and unprecedented. It lends itself to mental health challenges because no matter what teenagers have been led to believe, human beings NEED human interaction.

Dr. Melissa Mercado, a neurologist in Springfield Massachusetts, did a study on young girls at the beginning of the social media takeover and asserts the following:

"Theirs is a generation shaped by the smartphone and by the concomitant rise of social media. 'I call them iGen,'" she wrote. "The impact of these devices has not been fully appreciated, and goes far beyond the usual concerns about curtailed attention spans.   Rates of teen depression and

suicide have *skyrocketed* since 2011. In particular, self-inflicted injury rates for young females aged 10 to 14 years increased 18.8 percent *annually* from 2009 to 2015." Dr. Melissa Mercado, one of the authors of the study, told CBS News, "It's not an exaggeration to describe 'iGen' as being on the brink of the worst mental-health crisis in decades. Much of this deterioration can be traced to their phones."

WOW! Did you read that?! She said that self- inflicted injury rates for young females aged ten to fourteen years increased 18.8 percent *annually* from 2009 to 2015!!!!!!! That is an alarming statistic!!!!!

Dr. Mercado cites cyberbullying, fear and anxiety of being left out, and sleep deprivation tied to constant smartphone use as factors affecting teens' mental health and well-being. Cyber bullying is a particularly disturbing manifestation of the deteriorating mental health of Generations Y and Z. Traditional bullying occurred in the neighborhood, on the school bus, in class or the cafeteria. It was particularly traumatizing because bullying occurred in spaces that you could not avoid.

The reason that cyber bullying is so alarming is that it speaks to an addiction to social media that is so pervasive that the child will willingly submit themselves to verbal and emotional abuse rather than simply logging off. People are literally taking their own lives because of the 100% preventable issue of cyber bullying. How dysfunctional have we become as a society if children are suffering from deadly abuse but don't have the sense or the ability to simply disconnect from their abuser? This scenario is why it is critically important for you as a parent to be intimately involved in your child's life and emotional affairs.

There is a school of thought that advocates that the parent respect the child's independence and boundaries and allow them to have a level of privacy that the parent does not interfere with.

This philosophy is hogwash. Your child is your responsibility. While a healthy sense of independence is good, there should be NO SPACE in your child's life that is "off limits" to you as the parent. Do whatever you have to do to keep the lines of honest communication open with your child.

Among other findings, research showed that use of electronic devices including smartphones for at least five hours a day among teens more than doubled, from eight percent in 2009 to nineteen percent in 2015. The group who spent the most time glued to their phones were seventy percent more likely to have suicidal thoughts or actions than those who reported one hour of use per day.

We have to be diligent about understanding how technology is shaping our kids and then we must agree about how to deal with technology so that it doesn't rip the parents' relationship apart.

Your Adult "Kids"

This section could be a book on its own. The most critical thing to remember as you read this section is that you have raised your children and that you must love them while understanding that they have free will. Sometimes they WILL NOT make the same decision you would, or even anything remotely close to it. The key is to listen and let them know that you will always love them. This love should have some boundaries. For instance, you must be careful about co-signing major financial purchases and doing things for them that could adversely affect you and your spouse/partner in the future. However, keep the communication flowing. Sometimes your adult kids will not want your advice at all. They just may want to vent; they may be seeking your friendship, and that's okay. I am learning more and more that if I give advice before I am asked, giving unsolicited advice will just leave me and my wife frustrated. Oftentimes, we now have decided to be available, and let our kids know that we love them and that they always have a place to come back to, although my wife and I laugh and agree that that their return home should be temporary and not permanent.

The key is to get on one accord as the parents of the adult children as quickly as possible. Nothing will destroy a marriage or relationship faster than disagreement about how to handle your children, so make sure that you endeavor to agree.

Bonus Section: Your Aging Parents

My cousin Bertha used to constantly say, "We are either going to get old or die young." I never understood the statement until I began to watch my family members get older. Numerous things change with the aging process.

I know that many of you may not be at this stage yet, but as the old folks say, "Keep on living, baby." Additionally, if you are not at this stage yet, NOW is the perfect time to begin to prepare. If you and your parents live long enough, you may reach the point where you become caregivers to your elderly parents.

Typically, the responsibilities that you have will creep up on you over time, so it is important to start thinking about these responsibilities when one of two things happens: (1) your parents' health begin to decline (2) your parents begin to reach an age where they need more assistance.

I remember when my mom called me to let me know that she was diagnosed with Parkinson's disease. I was a 100% travel employee at that time and was planning to head back home for the weekend. Needless to say, those plans changed immediately, and back to New York I went to see my mom and to talk through what this responsibility would look like for our family. When things change for our aging parents, they change for us also. For this reason, consistent communication and agreement are essential in this process.

You and your spouse/significant other must have one mind about boundaries, expectations, and responsibilities.

First, I want to say to you, "Consider expanding your support network" immediately. If you have siblings, then everyone who is responsible, flexible, and mature will be needed to help. We were very fortunate that my aunt was retiring from her job and had time to provide "around the clock" care to my mom. Everyone contributed to the best of their ability, considering distance, time, and scheduling.

While you may not have had this conversation just yet, now is the perfect time to begin the discussion around a plan for the aging parent(s). I understand how difficult these thoughts can be, so I suggest that you start this conversation as early as possible and even consider speaking with a counselor. The benefit of having this difficult conversation early is that you can discuss very painful topics in a very abstract way. It is very difficult to discuss our roles and responsibilities for a sick parent while dealing with the pain of having a sick parent. It is much easier to have those caregiving conversations and to make those decisions while your parent is well and the conversation can more easily just be a "What if?" It can be earth-shattering to see the people who were so strong and full life begin to slow down. It can be mentally exhausting if you face a parent who develops dementia and he or she no longer knows who you are.

Consequently, you should learn your family's medical history and start talking to your parents as they age to know what health challenges they face in the future so that you can prepare together.

In our case, we had a delightful two years before Mom's health began to seriously decline. That period of time may not be the case with everyone. Just consider the conversation.

Finally, just as with the "newborn" example, be sure that if you end up with the full-time care of a parent or parents, you still make time for each other. You still need to do dates and vacations, even if the dates and vacations have to be closer to home than they usually would be.

If you strategically take care of the relationship, it will take care of you.

References:

https://www.todaysparent.com/family/how-babies-change-your-relationship/

https://ifstudies.org/blog/what-couples-with-children-argue-about-most/

https://kidshealth.org/en/parents/ adolescence.html

https://www.webmd.com/parenting/features/parenting-mistakes-teens#1

https://www.rd.com/advice/parenting/maintain-a-healthy-relationship-with-your-parents/

Bonus:

https://www.focusonthefamily.com/marriage/caring-for-aging-parents-and-your-marriage/

https://www.liveabout.com/rules-for-supporting-your-aging-parents-and-in-laws-2492347

Chapter 4

GROWN FOLK PROBLEMS

One of the most frustrating aspects of technology is that it is always changing. You only have only two choices: you can either keep up or be left behind!

While most people realize and accept the challenges of keeping up with an ever changing digital world, those same people somehow fail to understand that their romantic relationships function in the same way. Just as the apps on your devices are constantly sending you updates and "fixes," your relationship also requires constant maintenance AND constant adjustment on the part of both people in order for the relationship to remain healthy and functional. If you fail to download the latest updates to your device, your "apps" will eventually begin to experience problems, and they may eventually "crash."

Welcome to relationships.

LOVE

Throughout this book, the focused goal is to create and maintain a healthy and functional "operating system" in your relationship. However, if we are not intentional about downloading the updates as they become available, we can easily become vulnerable to viruses, bugs, and unexpected crashes in our relationships. Unlike our technological devices, our relationships rarely send us explicit messages that our relationship needs an update. But if we pay attention, we will see signals that indicate that our relationship has reached a point where we can no longer continue to operate in the way that has been successful in the past.

Consider these questions:

What updates have you missed in your relationship with spouse/partner?

Have you become so focused on *enjoying* your relationship that you have forgotten to do the required maintenance on it?

There's nothing more embarrassing than seeing a luxury car broken down on the side of the road because someone failed to do the basic maintenance required to keep it running. Here's the scary part, a problem that is totally preventable/fixable could wind up destroying your car if it is not dealt with in a timely manner.

For example, a leak in the engine coolant could be easily fixed. But if you ignore the warning signs, that simple, easily fixable problem could cause you to blow a head gasket, resulting of the need for an entirely new engine. I have counseled hundreds of couples over the years, and I have discovered that most relationships die from preventable diseases. Simply put, they didn't pay attention when they should have been downloading the latest update. They ignored the "service engine soon" light when it came on in their car, and now they are dealing with the inevitable result of negligence: Destruction.

WARNING!!!!

Maybe it's not your fault you missed the warning signs. Maybe you got so consumed with your career that you missed the warning signals. Maybe you missed the new sleep patterns, fragrance changes, clothing style upgrades, weight change, educational goal change, or anything else that indicates that your spouse or significant other's attention was being directed elsewhere. The sad reality is that countless couples have missed the warning signs that indicated that someone else has been able to slip into your partner's open emotional space because they needed an update in the relationship that you failed to provide.

I know that warning signs is a very emotional topic, but the reality is that a huge percentage of us very often miss our updates and end up spending countless hours trying to understand why the operating system in our marriage is breaking down.

Let me share a personal story.

My wife and I were married in our early twenties. After we were married, we immediately began our family. We had our first three children eleven months apart. For the first three years of our marriage, our journey consisted of baby feeding, diaper changing, and adjusting to very challenging sleep patterns. The thing is that we were on the same road with one direction. Our daily routines were quite set. We worked, maintained our home, attended night classes, focused on family, and attended church. We repeated this routine without variation, and repeated it weekly. We even managed to continue to navigate our lives through the eight month long leukemia battle, and eventually the death of our baby son. I think we did a very good job early in our marriage with paying attention to the signals and "downloading" the updates in our marriage.

About ten years into our marriage, however, I missed an update, and our marital operating system suffered because I was so distracted by what we all like to say is "vision" or "forward focus."

We all want to believe that we are on the path to making a better life for our families. We spend countless hours working, pursuing higher education, building self-empowerment, establishing various relationships, and spending more and more time away from our critical relationships with the intention of enhancing them. It's strange how we believe that works.

Having an Affair

The unfortunate part about marriage is that it becomes amazingly easy to be so in love with goals and vision that this preoccupation can potentially become an affair. It becomes easy to remove our attention away from our spouse/partner to our new "goals" (that totally exclude our spouse/partner) while at the same time convincing ourselves that our work is all being done so that we can have a better future for us and our family. We are destroying the foundation of our "present" in the name of building a legacy.

I remember so clearly the time when I had an "affair." And I'll never forget the advice that a wise and well-respected individual gave me. He said, "You need to leave your *girlfriend* alone and focus on your family." I was extremely insulted because I knew that I was committed and faithful to my marriage and that I was not allowing any extracurricular activities or individuals into my relationships. He saw the look on my face and proceeded to explain to me just what he was referring to. He explained to me that the "girlfriend" wasn't a person but rather a thing that I had picked up and made more of a priority than my wife and children.

I didn't even realize that I was so focused on this elusive goal that I thought would secure a better future for us —that I was missing out on the opportunity to include my wife on the journey which would have made the journey much more pleasurable. Remember that I mentioned in the previous chapter that I was raised by a strong, independently wealthy woman. For years, I watched her successfully download updates as a single person, which is totally different from having an operating system that includes two people. It's like a Mac versus a PC. Creating a successful life by yourself and creating a successful life with someone else are as different as night and day. My mistake was that I saw my mom "winning," so I unconsciously adopted a lot of her winning ways —not knowing that the same habits that helped her win in her life were helping me to lose in mine. I had no clue that I had adapted the same thought pattern and had become so involved with what I was doing that I completely missed the updates that would have directed my attention back to my wife.

So what about you? What has become your "side piece?" Who is your girlfriend/boyfriend? Have you allowed your career to get more of your heart, passion, and attention than your spouse? If so, are you ready to change?

Again, I know these are all loaded questions, but consider that when we continue to miss the updates and fail to make the necessary adjustments to our marital operating system, we subject our relationship to "bugs" and "crashes" which manifest themselves as arguments or dysfunction in our relationship. Not paying attention to these signs will lead to some very serious "grown-folk problems" in our relationship.

DEALING WITH CHANGE

Let's dive deeper into common changes that I like to call "Grown-Folk Problems:"

Friends

As we grow and evolve, so should our friendships. There are some friends from childhood that we love dearly, but they have not grown. These friends are still engaging in the same toxic and dysfunctional behaviors that they were practicing when we were kids. Unfortunately, we have carried these toxic friendships into our relationship with our spouse, and these toxic friendships are having a negative effect. If any association in your life is negatively affecting your marriage, you need to let it go. Period.

As we grow and evolve as human beings, we will inevitably develop new friendships. But sometimes the new friends we have acquired are accepted by only one person in the relationship. Your spouse/partner may tolerate them because of his/her love for you, but his/her instinct tells him/her that he/she is no good for you and his/her presence is causing a silent division. Again, if any association in your life is negatively affecting your marriage, you need to let it go.

As we navigate the very difficult challenge of growing together and making friends with couples that we *both* of enjoy, it is critically important to keep the lines of communication open. How do we feel about these new associations? What is it about this couple that we like/don't like? Where can we find people with similar values and interests?

Colleagues

Oftentimes we will develop work relationships with coworkers that continue after normal working hours. We will call them the "happy hour" colleagues. But in order to maintain a healthy relationship with these colleagues, here are some "updates" you need to look for:

- How far should this new friendship go?
- What new habits are being formed that no longer include your partner/spouse?
- Does it seem as if you enjoy their company more than coming home?
- Should your partner/spouse be your best friend?
- Where do we draw the line between maintaining a healthy individuality in your marriage and "growing apart"?

If you are not intentional about monitoring these updates as they present themselves, you will find yourself with an outdated or dysfunctional operating system in your marriage.

Business ventures

Sometimes in your marriage/relationship, you will come across unique chances to invest in opportunities to make some extra money through business ventures. But like everything else in your marriage, you need to do your due diligence before diving in and putting the family at risk.

Here are some questions your spouse/partner may ask that you need to be prepared for:

- Where did this idea come from?
- Did you invest in this business opportunity without discussing it with me first?
- What happened to our other financial goals?
- How do you know this business opportunity is going to work?

A huge key to getting your partner to accept this new business venture is for you to be intentional about welcoming all of their questions. If you get defensive and angry when your spouse starts asking legitimate questions about the offer/venture, your spouse will take that reaction as a sign that you have something to hide and will instantly assume that this business opportunity is not a worthy venture.

Career

One of the things that I always tell my wife is that "The worst thing that can happen is not for you to fail, but for you to succeed at making it to the top of the wrong ladder." A serious question that we all need to ask ourselves is "What happens when I succeed?" My wife and I have another adage that we quote often, "Everybody wants to be Beyoncé until it's time to do what Beyoncé does." Beyoncé Carter is one of the hardest working people on the planet. She is quoted as saying that one year she had only three days off: Christmas, her birthday, and some random other day. She worked 362 days that year. Needless to say, her husband had to make serious adjustments to his expectations of his wife during that time she was completely focused on her career. Unfortunately, as we all know, her husband Jay-Z wound up cheating on her during that time.

People see Beyoncé on stage, and they see the glamour and the lights, but the truth is that very few people *actually* want Beyoncé's life. The question is, "Now that you have advanced in your career, what does this success mean for your life, marriage, and mental health?"

- How many additional hours will you have to work?
- Will you have a secretary?
- How often will you have to travel?
- How much time will you devote to "date nights?" -How much time will you devote to spending time with the kids?
- Will you inadvertently wind up sacrificing your family on the altar of a successful career?

All of us know stories of people who were public successes and private failures. You do not want that to be your story. Public successes with private failures are one of the most critical areas for you to pay attention to the updates. If you miss too many of the updates, your operating system may crash and become unrecoverable.

Spirituality

I once did a poll amongst people who were married and those who were single. I asked, "How important is spirituality when choosing a mate?" The overwhelming majority said that it was *not* that serious and that it was not even a factor that they considered when choosing a mate. Overlooking spirituality is an egregious error. Whether you are a Christian, Jew, Muslim, Buddhist, Atheist, or Agnostic, your beliefs about

God (or lack thereof) will play a huge role in your marriage. Whether the spirituality entails tithing, church attendance, praying at home, or something else like drinking, smoking, extramarital affairs, or illegal activity, your value system will always play a role in how you solve conflict and how you handle difficult situations.

The purpose of this book is not to force any specific set of religious beliefs upon you, but it is to impress upon you the importance of being on the same page spiritually. Value systems matter, and they will always find a way to manifest themselves in a relationship. For example: If one of you believes in divine healing and one of you doesn't, then what do you do when one of the children gets really sick? If one of you believes in tithing and the other doesn't, then what do you do when one of you loses your job and you don't have enough money to pay your bills AND tithe? If one of you believes in going to church and the other one isn't greatly concerned about it, then what do you teach your children about the importance of church? How do you explain the fact that one parent attends every Sunday and the other parent doesn't attend at all?

Regardless of your views about the importance of spirituality in a marriage, I can assure you that it is very important. And if you and your spouse can't get on the same page spiritually, the success of your marriage may hang in the balance.

Family

As human beings, we are constantly growing and evolving. Even as individuals, it is hard to keep up with our own growth and development; therefore we must constantly check in with ourselves to make sure that we are okay. One of the major challenges about having a family is that you multiply those changes exponentially when you add a spouse and children. You must be diligent about constantly checking in with your family to stay on top of the updates.

What's New?

It is so easy to greet friends and familiar faces with the question, "What's New?" When was the last time that you asked your spouse/partner that question? When was the last time that you asked, -"What's changing with you?"

- "Where are you at in your headspace?"
- "What was the last change that happened that I may have missed?"

I know, more loaded questions, but I ask because over my years of counseling, these questions are a common thread of conversation that frequently comes up. Your spouse/partner has changed, and you totally missed the "update."

I remember experiencing several changes —personal changes —throughout my relationship with my wife: Something as simple as the thread count on our bedroom sheets or which type of fabric to use or lipstick colors or clothing preferences —all of these things could change in an instant, so I had to be on top of the update.

To be honest, change is usually not the problem. It is the *communication* of change (or the lack thereof) and the *adjustment* to change that typically causes the most challenges.

I remember seeing a sweater that I really liked. My wife asked me not to buy it because she wanted to buy it for me for the holiday. So I did what any good husband would do: I didn't buy it. The holiday rolled around, and I opened my gift box. I, somehow, just knew that it was the sweater that I wanted. My wife was extremely excited, but I was disappointed. I was disappointed because it was a *similar* sweater that she had found on sale at another store for less than half the price of the sweater I wanted. I didn't want to hurt her feelings, but I had to be honest in that moment. I let her know that I needed to return that sweater and that I would buy the one that I wanted. She asked, "Why? What's wrong with that one?" I let her know that the fabric and pattern was different and that the overall fit was not as tailored. Of course, that response led to a series of other questions. What I failed to communicate was that I had been trying on different styles to compliment my body type. This new practice had inevitably changed my taste in clothing. In short, I had downloaded a new update that I had failed to share with my wife.

This is a "sweater" example for us, but what change has taken place in your relationship —one that you may have missed? What old operating system no longer works because you have been exposed to something different? What updates have you or your partner missed?

As human beings, we are always growing, changing, and evolving. It is extremely critical that we keep up with the changes, specifically those in our significant others. I know that we can easily get distracted with work, life, social media, and outside obligations, but it is critical to the success of your union that you keep your eyes on the home front so that you can adjust to the changes that are sure to happen. If you pay attention and intentionally adjust to all of the updates, you will be able to deal with your "Grown Folks" problems!

Chapter 5

MONEY TALK

Even though problems with "Money Talk" qualify as "Grown-Folks Problems," I thought that this topic deserved its own chapter.

Everyone has a money story. Some stories are filled with opulence and abundance, some are conservative, and some are just downright embarrassing. Just know that there is a conversation that must occur in all three of the above mentioned categories for any relationship to be healthy. Also, one should note that "Money Talk" is not a onetime conversation. The "Money Talk" should definitely happen in the beginning of the relationship, but it should also evolve throughout the course of your marriage. One initial conversation will not suffice because life and financial statuses will change with age and experiences.

Let's identify the three commonly-known money statuses for the sake of the information that will be discussed throughout this chapter.

UPPER, MIDDLE, AND LOWER CLASS

Upper Class- In 2020, the Pew Research Center defines *Upper Class* as someone who makes at least $78,281.00 as a single person or at least

$156,561.00 for a family of four. In order to translate this information into a practical application, however, the cost of living in your individual city must be taken into account. An income of $78,000.00 will create an entirely different life in Greensboro, NC, than it will in San Francisco, California.

Middle Class - In 2020, the Pew Research Center defines *Middle Class* as someone who makes at least $26,093 as a single person or at least $52,187.00 for a household of four.

Lower Class/Poverty- Anyone making less than any of the amounts listed above for their category is technically in poverty.

How to Win with Money in your Marriage

There are three critical aspects to winning the money game in your marriage:

1. Communication
2. Agreement
3. Trust

Communication

First, you must be willing to talk about financial issues. It is amazing to me how many couples never discuss debt, financial goals, credit scores, saving versus spending, etc., before they commit to being in a serious, long-term relationships with one another. You will never confront and master anything you are not first willing to have a conversation about.

Agreement

Next, you need to have agreement. If one of you wants to live in a mansion, but your partner wants to live in a townhome, you guys are not in agreement about the amount of money that needs to be spent on housing, which means that you probably have conflicting ideas about quality of life. In her book "Break Up of Make Up," author Rainah Davis explains to couples that lifestyle and money choices are a window into the realm of compatibility. She shares her story of how she and her children lived in seven different homes in an eight-year period because her ex-husband was determined to live in homes that they simply could not afford. Davis stated that there was constant disagreement over every dollar that came into the house because the couple was "house poor." They were spending between

50-60% of their income on housing, and because some of the larger of these homes spanned from 3,000-6,000 square feet, their utilities were astronomical. She explains that her unwillingness to live without a true quality of life for her and her four children was one of the major reasons for her marriage "break up."

She is not unique. Unfortunately many of us know people who suffer because of a spouse who overspends or constantly takes on more and more debt until the couple is drowning in bills. And unless you and your significant other have agreement to "fake it until you make it," then you are setting yourself up for trouble.

Trust

Finally, you must have trust. You are not going to be with your partner every single moment of the day. You have to be able to trust their decision-making process. And you if you are the spender, you may want to just ask for an allowance account upfront so that you do not put the household in jeopardy.

BABY STEPS

At the beginning of my relationship before marriage, I was aware that I personally fell into the middle class category. I was not rich by a long shot, but by the grace of God, I was not in extreme poverty either.

My mom demonstrated a very strong work ethic. She owned several properties and was wise with investing. One of her favorite phrases was, "You have the power when you have your own key."

Mom was letting me know that decisions are easier to make when you can leverage the power of ownership. You have the key, so you get to make the decisions.

I was fifteen years old when I got my first real job. My mom used to use the time that we were in the car on the way to the bank to talk to me about the financial principles that would shape my perspective on money forever. My mom was clear with me. She would say, "We will not be spending this entire check. We will tithe (take 10% for charitable giving), we will save, we will pay your beeper bill; and then you can have twenty dollars to spend however you like!" My mother provided very solid direction. Her plan was foolproof for me as a teenager. My mom ensured that I had the basics that I needed to be financially successful early.

My late uncle often said, "Your mother is the first female millionaire that I've known personally, but she won't admit it." My uncle would further let me know how much I could benefit from both her wisdom and generosity. Although my mom was very quiet in manner, she was wealthy in wisdom.

Now that you know that information about my life, it's quite clear that I knew where I stood as an individual before inviting someone else into my money world. This clarity is important for you also. You must be honest about where you are so that you can establish what your financial focus and agreement will be as you set the course for your life together.

I come from an extremely generous family, so giving was a huge part of me. I was clear that anyone I was dating had to be okay with me being generous with my/our money. Growing up, we had a running joke that our house was the gathering place for anyone who needed shelter, food, clothing, money, furniture, and the list goes on. I can't even begin to remember the entire list of things that we have given away as a family.

Now consider this information: my mom was a separated woman who raised four biological children and two grandchildren on her income alone. I reflect often on just how amazing she was to work two jobs to ensure that the home was taken care of while she was accomplishing so many of her goals.

I share that information with you because my wife's upbringing was the total opposite. Her family was very conservative and private. Sharing and big gatherings were not a common practice in their home. My mother-in-love and wife were often shocked at how many needy people my family would have in and out of our home at any given time.

My wife and her family couldn't understand why we felt the need to help others and have an open door at all times.

For my wife and I, these were two extreme and opposite views. Finally, we had to find a happy medium. We had to find a compromise so that I wouldn't suffer from the lack of family and friend interaction that I was accustomed to from my upbringings and so that she would not feel overwhelmed by the amount of people that were in and around our home at any given time.

Honestly, we did not hit a solid agreement on helping family and friends until about three years into our marriage when our son was diagnosed with leukemia. That diagnosis changed so many things for us by default. We didn't have a choice as we had two other children who needed to be cared for as we went back and forth to the hospital with our ill son. This lesson helped my wife to let her guard down and become open to accepting more than just those of us in our house.

As the years progressed, we worked until we found a happy medium. I am happy to say that our home is probably one of the busiest homes on our street as the family's kids come through often and family comes to visit with us often. What's more, my wife couldn't be happier to see everyone together. It took years to get to this place. Please be sure to give careful attention to what you and your partner/spouse can agree on.

This is all important for this chapter because our views of money are shaped in our home first, and if not properly discussed, this could be a significant reason for constant anger, communication breakdowns, separation and even divorce.

THE SECOND LEADING CAUSE FOR DIVORCE IN AMERICA

If we were playing the game "Family Feud," and the question was:

"What is second leading cause of divorce in America behind infidelity?"

What would your answer be?

If you guessed, "Finances," you would be correct! Maybe that question was a little too easy considering that money is the subject of this chapter. Still, isn't it scary just how many marriages end up in divorce because of financial stress, issues, and miscommunication?

Can you remember the last *intense* conversation that you and your spouse had about money? Did it turn into an argument? Did it ever get resolved? Did you both just avoid the conversation because of different views?

Let me share some irony with you about unresolved conflict in marriage. One of the greatest aspects of marriage is that marriage gives you the opportunity to spend a lifetime with someone while creating memories that they will never forget. But do you know what one of the *worst* things about marriage is? It forces you to spend a lifetime with someone creating memories that they will never forget! Yes, this aspect of marriage can be a blessing and a curse, and that is what makes unresolved conflict so poisonous to long-term relationships. If you've ever had a serious money disagreement with your spouse that never became resolved, do yourself a favor, and revisit it now. Few issues are more frustrating and potentially volatile in a relationship than dealing with the pain and trauma of a recurring fight about money.

I can remember it as if it was yesterday. Many years ago, very early in our marriage, I was convinced that it was time to begin a new business venture. My wife was totally supportive since I was in a full-time travel position for work, and she could use more assistance at home during the week with our three young children. As my wife began to ask additional questions and dig deeper, the conversation became more intense. Her questions about start-up costs, my current salary, home finance, and potential failure of this new venture began to irritate me because I thought I had covered all of her questions in my presentation.

Talk about an intense conversation!

The question that struck a nerve was, "What if it doesn't work?"

I had spent months speaking with mentors about this venture's prospects. Moreover, people whom I respected had stepped out and built their businesses. After my twelve-hour workday, I spent each night in my hotel room digging and searching to gather information to share with my wife at what I believed was the right time. Can you imagine trying to gather information on slow dial-up internet? Can you imagine the frustration of trying to research —only to be kicked offline if the phone rang, necessitating having to begin the search again? Do you remember the time when cell phones operated by minutes? There was no such thing as plans that gave you unlimited minutes because the whole cell phone idea was still very new at that time. I think you get my point. Loads of energy and time went into gathering pertinent information.

My wife and I went from zero to one hundred within a twenty minute timeframe. It turned into an argument about money. But the truth is that the argument *wasn't* about money; it was about security.

> *Money is always an intense topic because money represents security.*

While my wife is usually supportive of the decisions that I make for our family, at that particular point in our financial journey, our family's financial security could have potentially been affected by this venture. The hard, solid truth was that the concept was amazing and would've worked well, but the timing wasn't right. And in business as well as in life, *timing* is everything. Do you know what the only difference is between a strike and a home run? Timing. The right thing at the wrong time is the wrong thing.

Simply put, even though this business venture was an appealing idea, my wife and I couldn't afford the risk associated with launching a new business venture at the time.

I share this story with you because over the years, I have spent countless hours speaking with couples who have been having intense conversations, arguing, and even ready to separate because of disagreements over money decisions. In most cases, the issue is not the lack of money; it was the lack of financial agreement due to an inability to agree on the path toward financial security.

Your challenge could be totally different. Consider the following money conversations that you and your spouse/partner may have had:

Your partner/spouse likes to spend, and you like to save.

Your partner/spouse prefers an apartment downtown with a view overlooking the city while you prefer a house built in the country from the ground up.

You prefer private school while your spouse prefers public school.

You like charitable giving, and your spouse/ partner sees it as money thrown out of the window.

The preference list provided above could continue indefinitely, yet the truth remains that money will always be a "sore spot" in your marriage until you and your spouse/partner establish a "financial security agreement."

How can we establish an agreement so that every conversation we have about money becomes less intense? I'm glad you asked. Here's the Blueprint:

FINANCIAL SECURITY AGREEMENT

1. Assets and Liabilities: Talk about what you *own* and what you *owe*.

    Assets include, but are not limited to:

    - Savings
    - Property
    - Investments Businesses

    Liabilities include but are not limited to:

    - Credit card debt/Line of Credit Mortgages
    - Car loans
    - Student loans
    - Personal loans

2. Credit: What's Your Score?

   Most people have less than perfect credit. While it is not a deal breaker for most people, poor credit DOES affect the marriage. If you have a low score, what are your plans to improve it?

3. Shared Financial Goals: Where are you headed financially as a couple?

   What do you want to accomplish? For example, you may want to:

   Create an emergency savings account
   - Buy a home.
   - Pay off all of your debt.
   - Take a dream vacation.
   - Save for retirement.
   - Create an investment portfolio.
   - Buy a car.
   - Have children.

   In order to reach your shared financial goals, you must:
   - Write them down.
   - Put them in order of importance.
   - Plan how much money you will need for each goal.
   - Create and constantly revisit your budget as a couple to see if there are ways to increase your savings.
   - Decide how much you will both contribute to your financial goals per month.

4. Money Language. Just as we all have a love language (the way we express, receive, and relate to love), we all have a "Money

Language" (the way we earn, spend and think about money). And just like conflicting love languages, conflicting money languages will wreak havoc on your relationship. Here are some questions to ask to determine your money language:

- Do you have a budget?
- Are you the type of person who finds it easy to make a budget and stick to it?
- What are the "needs" and "wants" reflected in your budget? Are you aware of which items fall into which categories?
- Do you typically save for major purchases, or do you borrow?
- What do you typically spend a good deal of money on?
- What did your parents teach you about money?
- Did your parents abide by their own money rules, or did you ever see them breaking them?
- In your opinion, is money hard or easy to come by?
- Did your parents teach you that "Money doesn't grow on trees"?
- Were you taught that money was the root of all evil?
- Do you believe that rich people gain their wealth by stealing from or exploiting the poor?
- Do you find yourself stressing about bills, unexpected expenses, or other financial matters?

The purpose of asking these questions is not to attack your spouse for having a different value system than you when it comes to money matters. The purpose of this conversation is to discover what your spouse's money language is and then to work on finding a system that works for both of you.

5. Financial Roles

   It is impossible to have a good team if you don't have good individual players. And it is impossible to have good individual players if everyone doesn't know how to play their position well. Teamwork is extremely important in a relationship because in order for your relationship to work, there must be a successful balance.

   Here are some helpful questions to ask as you determine your financial roles.

   - Who pays the bills? How did you come to this conclusion?
   - Who paid the bills in your household while you were growing up? How did that model work for your parents? Do you want to keep or reject that model for your family?
   - Is it possible to share bills? If so, how? Do you split them down the middle?
   - Does the person who makes the most money automatically pay the lion's share of the bills? Or do we create an equal system, regardless of income?
   - Is the person who makes the money automatically responsible for actually paying the bills?
   - Which one of you is the more organized person?
   - Who is more technologically savvy and better suited for paying bills and keeping records online?

   These are just a few of the questions that you can ask to get your financial security agreement started. Keep in mind that financial roles may change, depending on the financial status of either spouse. Bear in mind that people lose jobs, get raises/promotions, and have all types of changes in their financial status over the years. I cannot stress enough that just as if everything else we have discussed, you must continue to revisit the topic of financial roles in order to ensure that everything continues to run as optimally as possible for as long as possible.

STARTING THE MONEY TALK

If you're nervous about having a money conversation with your spouse, here is a formula to help you get the conversation started:

The Plan: Get your partner's opinion about someone *else's* financial situation.

The Script: "My dad is thinking about putting this bill on his credit card, but he already has a lot of debt. What do you think he should do?"

The Rationale: People are always more comfortable discussing other people's problems than they are their own. Framing the question in this way creates emotional distance for your partner and allows them to view the issue more objectively instead of immediately reacting out of personal fear.

You can fix your money problems

If you find yourself having challenges in the money department of your marriage. One of the most important points to realize is that you are not alone. In 2018, Dave

Ramsey's company, "Ramsey Solutions," released some mind-blowing statistics relating to money in marriage.

First, the organization reported that: "The number one issue couples fight about is also a topic many couples avoid discussing —money. According to a survey by Ramsey Solutions, results show that both high levels of debt and a lack of communication are major causes for the stress and anxiety surrounding household finances."

The survey also shared these findings:

- Nearly two-thirds of all marriages start off in debt. Forty-three percent of couples married more than twenty-five years started off in debt, while eighty-six percent of couples married five years or less started off in the red —twice the number of their older counterparts.
- One-third of people who say they have argued with their spouse about money say that they had hidden a purchase from their spouse because they knew their partner would not approve.
- Ninety-four percent of respondents who say they have a "great" marriage discuss their money dreams with their spouse, compared to only forty-five percent of respondents who say their marriage is "okay" or "in crisis." Eighty-seven percent of respondents who say their marriage is "great" also say they and their spouse work together to set long-term goals for their money.
- Sixty-three percent of those with $50,000 or more in debt feel anxious about talking about their personal finances. Forty-seven percent (almost half) of respondents with consumer debt say that their level of debt creates stress and anxiety.

Let's break this idea down further. First of all, based on this research, there is no wonder that relationships are in such distress! If marriages start off in debt with no plan to attack the debt and eliminate it is a major hurdle to overcome.

The next statistic about partners hiding finances is a gigantic issue! And these are not just statistics because I have counseled couples who have bank accounts that their spouse does not even know about. I am not talking about separate accounts that the couple have agreed upon, I am talking about secret, hidden accounts. Some people were even *taught* to hide finances from their partners by their family members. Some women were raised to believe that they needed to have a rainy-day fund just in case their husband "acts up." Maybe you have never heard that advice given, but I surely have, and if someone feels the need to have an "escape fund," he or she probably is not a person who should be committing to spend his or her life in covenant with someone else. I am not against couples having separate accounts per se, but I *am* against couples having secrets because a secret never remains a secret forever. Inevitably, a situation arises that reveals the hidden account. And that is when things get interesting...

The other reason that "hiding money and purchases" is such a big issue is that hiding finances leads to a term that I was just introduced to a couple of years ago, called "marital infidelity." No, it's not what you're thinking! A 2016 Forbes article defines "marital infidelity" as "cheating" on a spouse by not disclosing money secrets.

That same article (a 2016 Harris poll for the National Endowment for Financial Education) revealed that 42% of Americans *admit* to deceiving their spouses financially. WOW. And that's not all. This number is actually 33% higher than it was two years ago. Financial deceit is a serious issue because it speaks to a lack of trust in your partner. According to New York-based psychotherapist Katherine Schafler, you can gauge the severity of financial infidelity and its consequences through the amount of spending involved, and the efforts to keep the financial infidelity hidden.

All of these concerns are factors because in a relationship, trust is essential. I maintain that if you cannot trust a person with your money, you should think long and hard about whether you want to trust them with the rest of your life. And even if the answer is yes, you should still have at-length conversations about who will be responsible for the financial decisions. And if one person is clearly better with handling the finances, that person should be in charge. Regardless of traditional gender roles and in spite of who the "breadwinner" is in the marriage, the person who is more financially astute should be handling your books.

The Money Talk

Here are some conversations that I suggest you have. They will be uncomfortable, but you both will be thankful as you begin to unwrap financial details which will become great teaching tools for other couples you will encounter later.

1. Family planning

    Have conversations about the cost of children. I know it sounds a little weird, but how much will each child cost from birth to college graduation? What will raising a child cost in terms of time and money commitment. Remember: we often say that "time is money."

I believe that the days are gone of adding a little water to the soup to make the soup "stretch." As the world advances, it becomes even more essential to have a financial plan for everything, especially for raising children.

2. Life Insurance

Do you have life insurance? How many policies do you have? How much do they cost monthly/ annually? Who is the beneficiary? Are you willing to change it or them? Why or why not? How much is the policy worth? Is it term or whole life? Have you borrowed from the policy? If yes, how much?

3. Education

What is the highest level of education you have completed? Do you think that you will be pursuing another degree?

If we have/adopt children, will they attend public school or private school?

What is our budget for the household educational future?

Are we paying cash for tuition, hoping for scholarships, taking out loans, or cashing in some of the investments?

4. Investments

Do you have any investments? Do you have stocks, bonds, IRA's, mutual funds, property/ properties, additional accounts? Whose names are listed as the beneficiaries for each of the above-mentioned? What is the value? Do you need to hold on to them, or is it time to sell/cash? Are you the sole individual on these investments?

5. Businesses

   Do we have any business ventures that interest us? Is there anything we can create that will generate income for the family —either residual or otherwise?

6. Taxes

   Do you owe any back taxes?

7. Bank Accounts

   Do you believe in separate bank accounts or shared accounts? Do you believe in mattress money saving? How many accounts do you have now? Where do you bank?

   Let's discuss your current interest rates. Do you have credit card debt connected to your bank account? What are your auto drafts?

8. Debt

   Do you have credit cards? Are they secured or unsecured? What are your limits? How much do you currently owe? Do you pay your bills on time? Are all of your interest rates extremely high?

   What is your credit score like? When was the last time you checked it? What is an acceptable score in your opinion? If your score is unacceptable, what are you doing to change it?

   There was a couple whose husband wasn't working, but the wife was. The husband was a former military man and had taken advantage of the GI Bill, which gave him money for college. Unbeknown to his wife, he had fraudulently cashed a tuition check, even though he wasn't in school that semester. When the wife filed her taxes, the government took thousands of dollars out of HER refund in order to pay for his debt. Needless to say, this unaccounted for debt put a strain on the marriage.

9. Property

   Do you own any property? What's the value? What's the balance? Have you borrowed on the property? Do you plan to buy together? Do you plan to rent? If yes, how long will you rent? What is your mortgage/rent budget? What is most important: location, cost, design? Do you need to live close to family? If yes, how close and whose family?

10. Travel and Vacations: How often? Location? Budget?

    How many vacations will you take each year? Will you take mini trips in-between? How often will you visit family and close friends that are not local?

    How often will you travel internationally? Will you travel with any charitable organizations? How much will you budget for each trip? How will you negotiate holidays? Which holidays will you spend with your family? Which holiday will you spend with your spouse's family?

    Are there certain holidays that are more important to your family than others? For instance, I know of a couple who split up Thanksgiving and Christmas because Thanksgiving was extremely important to the wife's family while Christmas was important to the husband's family. Whatever you ultimately decide, it is extremely important to have this discussion BEFORE the holidays. Holidays are an emotional time and it can potentially cause major issues if the holidays catch you without an agreed-upon plan.

11. Pre-Nuptial Agreements:

    Does either of you find them necessary? Why? What will be included in the "pre-nup? Who will be responsible for the cost associated with establishing this agreement?

References:

https://www.forbes.com/sites/vanessamcgrady/2016/06/02/infidelity/#d88bef63735d

https://www.marriage.com/advice/finance/finances-in-marriage/

https://www.daveramsey.com/pr/money-ruining-marriages-in-America

Chapter 6

IS IT WORTH IT?

It is very easy to be committed to anything for a short time. However, when we consider the challenges of long term commitment that is a totally different story.

When we consider the wedding vows that have been taken or in some cases will be taken, here are a few lines you will commonly hear:

"For richer or poorer, in sickness and in health, until death do you part"

While this vow sounds easy and mushy in front of your audience, the reality will soon impact the life-long commitment that you have just made in front of your family and friends. And nothing can test that commitment quite like a major crisis.

MARRIAGE CRISIS

"A marriage crisis typically occurs when an unusual amount of stress or unresolved conflict causes the level of anxiety to become too intense for the couple to manage. As a result, anger, resentment, dissatisfaction, frustration, and hopelessness take control of the relationship. The couple typically continues the negative interactions —or disengages completely from one another, and the relationship shuts down. I call this the boiling point or marital meltdown in the

marriage. (Mitch Temple, from Focus on the Family article, "Is Your Marriage in Crisis?")

The best thing that a couple can do for their marriage when problems negatively over-shadow the good, is to seek counseling as quickly as possible. The more time that passes, the greater the damage. If problems progress to the point of threatening the life of the marital union, special treatment is required to stabilize things — STAT! And even then, it's very difficult to turn things around in a positive direction. However, it IS possible.

There are several types of marital crises. Over the next few pages, we will discuss some of the main ones.

THE TERMINAL ILLNESS CRISIS

Couples who stay together long enough have their own rhythm and their own tempo that glide them through life. Just like a spicy salsa or a captivating waltz, there is something about watching couples move through life to the beat of their own drum.

There are few things that can throw off a couple's rhythm like a health scare or terminal illness. In an instant, the music stops, and everything is different. All of a sudden, the couple is forced to embrace change. But change, in itself, does not have to be completely negative. When change is approached properly, change actually creates an opportunity for growth.

In the beginning of this book there is a quote about the Chinese word for *Crisis*. While the strict etymology is debatable, it, nonetheless, proves a valid point. Every crisis that you face is both a danger to you and an opportunity for you.

Couples who see chronic illness as a shared challenge can find opportunities to connect with one another that are new and satisfying.

When you face an illness that hits you or your significant other out of the blue, it can certainly rock you both to your core. Since art imitates life, I can give you an example from the TNT series called Murder in the First. It is an American detective drama television series that was created by Steven Bochco and Eric Lodal and starred Taye Diggs and Kathleen Robertson as the leading detectives.

The very first show of the season shows Taye Diggs' character at the bedside of his dying wife. The doctor comes in and asks to speak with him; Afterwards, the husband and attending physician they step into the hallway, and the doctor lets Diggs know that there is nothing more to do. The doctor suggests that Diggs take his wife home so that she can be with him for the last time on Earth. But Diggs begs the doctor to try another treatment. In turn, the doctor says to the husband that she has fought hard for Diggs and put up a good fight, and that in return, Diggs needed to do something for her and "let her go."

Later in that episode Diggs' dying wife expresses that although she is the one dying, she feels the spouse that has the most difficult time is the healthy one. At some point, the patient makes their peace with their mortality, while the other mate is left with the pain of the tragic passing of the other.

My own personal struggle

I can remember as though it were yesterday. I was sitting on the couch eating Chinese food at 9:11pm on a Sunday night when the gastrointestinal doctor shared the results from my recent visit to his office. For years, I would often choke when trying to swallow certain food items, even after chewing what seemed like a thousand times. I am not exaggerating. He called to let me know that he had biopsied a sample of the tumor he found in my esophagus and had sent it to the gastro-oncology department for analysis. He was informed that I had a form of cancer in my small intestine which was causing the choking. The cancer was growing and needed to be removed immediately. Talk about a shock! My wife and I listened to all of the information presented to us on the following Tuesday and began preparation for the necessary surgery to remove the cancer. Due to the location of the cancer, it was important to move quickly to avoid additional spreading.

The surgery went very well, and I survived with a nice line down the middle of my stomach. But hey, I'm cancer free. My recovery was challenging. It took almost a year to get back to

normal. This process could not be rushed, no matter how hard I tried (and trust me, I tried). Talk about an unexpected crisis! We had no thoughts that in my early 40's I would be dealing with any type of cancer. I worked out daily, tried to eat as healthfully as possible, even with a serious sweet tooth, and I was very consistent with doctor's appointments and follow-ups. In fact, the surgeon even mentioned that good health was favorably on my side or that operation, which otherwise would have been very different.

I share this information with you because my diagnosis was definitely an opportunity for my wife to ask herself, "Is it worth it?" Cancer seems like a death sentence to most of us. At best, we can remain in remission while fearing the threat of a return at any moment. Every checkup can make us extremely nervous. My recovery was long, and required frequent visits to the emergency room and several extended stays at the hospital. It was the time to trade me in for a younger model; to get a newer version with no bruises or threats of a recurrence. Instead, she asked herself the question, "Is it worth it?"

Something to ponder when we have invested a generous amount of time in a relationship is that there will come a time when we will have to ask ourselves this nagging question. My hope is that your answer will be "Yes."

PTSD

Post-Traumatic Stress Disorder (PTSD) is a common after-effect of crisis. When we think of the term, we typically think of a soldier who has been to war or a child who has been abused, but we seldom think of PTSD in terms of a couple who has been through trauma. Sadly, many of relationships are not only dealing with PTSD, but they've been dealing with it for so long that they have come to accept it as their "new normal."

A tragedy such as a death, miscarriage, loss of employment or home, serious illness, or other catastrophic event is challenging, even for the best of relationships. If our relationship has not been as strong as it could be, a life crisis will hit us even harder. Sometimes couples shut down in their grief or deny blame for one another about what has happened. Sometimes they grieve in different ways and misread one another. For example, a husband who returns to work the day after a stillborn experience and a wife is left in disbelief, mistakenly assuming that her husband does not care.

We handle trauma in our own individual ways and sometimes our ways clash, leaving us feeling alone and unsupported. We will help you talk to each other about what the traumatic event has meant to you. We will establish some agreed upon ways that you can be there for one another and show support, whether it be talking or building some reliable rituals of connection. Facing a tragedy is never easy but facing it alone can feel devastating. Don't let a traumatic event come between you. Couples counseling can help.

When your marriage or relationship has been through a crisis, you may not feel connected with one another, even when you aren't arguing. The friendship may feel "flat" or nonexistent, and discussions about differences may be polarizing, that is, if you are engaging with one another at all. THIS IS NOT NORMAL. These are all signs that something is seriously wrong in your relationship.

THE AFFAIR CRISIS

An extramarital affair is considered by most partners to be a profound betrayal. In her book *Not Just Friends*, Dr. Shirley Glass uses the metaphor of walls and windows to describe what happens when an affair takes place. "In a love affair, the unfaithful partner has built a wall to shut out the marriage partner and has opened a window to let in the affair partner. To re-establish a marriage that is intimate and trusting after an affair, the wall and the window must be reconstructed to conform to the safety code which keeps the structure of the marriage sound enough to withstand the test of time."

Sometimes affairs are physical, and sometimes they are emotional. Affairs can be heterosexual or homosexual. They can occur at work, church, while volunteering with civic organizations, or during any other time that you spend away from your spouse. The one thing that all types of affairs have in common is that they are all destructive.

Continuing Dr. Glass's "wall" metaphor, when/if an affair happens, it is important to repair the wall that protects your marriage and create a strong boundary between you and the offended partner. Repairing the wall means ending the affair and agreeing to no more secrets. Once you understand what happened with both partners in the know, we can begin to look at rebuilding the trust and foundation of the relationship. Although affairs are serious, they are not the real reason that couples get divorced. The word "infidelity" literally means "unfaithful" or "not trustworthy." It is the breach of trust that couples struggle to repair and leads to divorce.

THE "GROWING APART" CRISIS

The "disengaged" couple is actually at the highest risk for divorce. In a study by The Divorce Mediation Project, 80% of men and women listed gradually growing apart, losing a sense of closeness, and not feeling loved and appreciated as reasons for initiating divorce. While there are many reasons for feeling isolated and lonely, they can all lead to serious danger for your marriage —not because of what you are feeling, but because of what you are not feeling. All couples (no matter how in love you are) are at risk for this crisis. I often tell couples: "Couples 'grow apart' all the time. As human beings, we naturally grow and evolve. And as life changes, so do we. The only thing that you have to do to 'grow apart' is not to be intentional about 'growing together.'"

The lost connection that leads to growing apart is typically caused by the small but significant ways that couples have turned away or against one another over time. The task for both of you is to create a safer, more secure marital/partnered environment where you are willing and free again to take some emotional risks.

THE ABUSE CRISIS

If you are experiencing substance abuse or domestic violence in your relationship, it is crucial that you get help right away. You should seek a professional and give the professional a complete history from both of you to see how best to approach treatment. Depending on the severity of the problem, couples' counseling may or may not be appropriate. If your spouse is hitting, raping, or otherwise abusing you in any way, then you should immediately remove yourself physically from the situation. Just because someone loves you doesn't mean that they are not still sick and/ or dangerous.

I have counseled numerous couples' relationships in which one spouse told the abuser that the abuser's behavior was "unacceptable," but the spouse still stayed. If you are still *accepting* the behavior, then there is no way to communicate to the abuser that the behavior is unacceptable. Have enough respect for yourself and your marriage to leave immediately, and demand that the spouse undergo psychological treatment before agreeing to return.

The "Romance after Death" Crisis

While I have not had to experience this crisis personally, I have had the opportunity to walk with several individuals through this particular experience. Each person explains it differently, yet the thing they all have in common is that they will never find a spouse/partner quite like the one they had. We walk through the process. We talk about all the things that the spouse/partner provided and didn't provide. We talk about the current needs. The needs always vary: financial, sexual, companionship, child rearing, home stability, investments, blended families, and appropriate next steps. As you are seeing, there are so many things that one has to consider after the death of a spouse/partner.

Reader, consider this common statement: I don't know if I will ever find anyone like "spouse/partner's name here."

When we begin this conversation, we walk through what an ideal spouse would look like at this juncture of their lives. Of course, the amount of time they were married along with the above-mentioned items come into play, but is important is the question: "What do you want now?" Part of dating after the death of a spouse is fully allowing the grieving process to take place and becoming aware of who you are as an individual and the person that you have become.

As you read in Chapter 2, there were some things that you and your spouse/partner missed about one another, and this may be the opportunity to ensure that you pay attention to this stuff up front. Death is painful and eye opening. It also forces one to look within. When we look within, we realize that we are a serious candidate for dating, or that no; not the time for me just yet.

I remember one person in particular and saying to myself that this person seems to too good to be true. It's like he or she has been waiting for me all this time. He or she is so different from my previous partner; I'm not even sure if I can measure up. My partner accepted me as I was; we were together for what seemed like forever. This was the best opportunity to explore this conversation even more. Sometimes, a person seems too good to be true because we have only had one thing for years at a time without a reason to pull on the creative side of ourselves which opens us up to new.

When they begin to consider it from that angle, it totally shifted their thinking. They then realized that yes, it's scary and different, but the potential relationship is worth "going for it."

It's extremely important that you think and talk thoroughly through this process so that you can make the best decisions.

SOLUTIONS

Before we go further on this topic, if you are serious about FIXING the crisis in your marriage then you need to make the following commitment to yourself and to your spouse:

"I am taking away the option of Divorce."

Make a commitment never to even say the "D" word. Remove it from your vocabulary and your mind as often as it tries to come up. If you don't make this commitment, it will just drain you of the energy that you need to put forth to save your marriage.

The truth is that marital crises can produce a relentless onslaught on your brain while it is trying to tempt you to give up. But the key is not to let it get the best of you. Don't allow negative thoughts to hinder your ability and motivation to turn things around in a good direction. Don't give in to the temptation to just give up.

"You've probably heard of the old military expression, "Surrender is not an option." When a ship's captain headed into battle where surrender wasn't an option, he would give the order to nail his country's colors to the mast. After the flags were nailed up high, during the battle, there was just no way to lower them and run up the flag of surrender. When the crew realized that there was no option but to fight, they became more determined to win the battle. This determination is the same mindset we're to have in marriage. Our one option in marriage is to stand our ground, to fight off the forces that would separate us from one another, and find a way to make the relationship work" (Dr. Norm Wright, from the book, One Marriage Under God).

Now that we've gotten that out of the way, here are some guidelines to help you navigate your marital crises.

—BONUS MATERIAL!!!!!!—

EMERGENCY CRISIS PROCEDURES FOR YOUR MARRIAGE:

1. **Be intentional in having an "emergency mindset."**

What is an emergency mindset? It is a state in which you recognize that you are in a crisis situation that could lead to the death of your marriage. You must commit to doing whatever is required to stabilize the situation first. You don't go back to the car for the insurance papers while the patient is "bleeding out." Afterward, it will be important to work on individual problems one-by-one, seeking the best "medicine" and help possible, even bringing in "doctors" when necessary. But first, you must acknowledge that you are in a crisis.

"Just as the person experiencing acute medical distress needs special care, a couple in crisis also needs special treatment. When a person suffers from a severe medical condition, the medic or emergency room doctor doesn't spend hours gathering a comprehensive patient history. The medical personnel need specific information to stabilize the immediate situation. Long-range decisions can be made later. Long-range plans are irrelevant if the patient is dead. The same analogy fits the marriage in crisis" *(David Hawkins, Ph.D)*.

Don't ignore or downplay what could happen if you aren't intentional in your actions. Don't just look at *"how to"* do what is necessary. Work on having the *"heart to"* do what is necessary. If you have the "heart to" do what is needed, you will be open to looking for "how to" do what is needed ... and then actually DOING it.

2. **Take yourselves to the best emergency room possible, as quickly as possible.**

In the same way that you would take a bleeding patient to an emergency room and clear the room of anyone else who may complicate matters, you should take the same measures for your bleeding marriage. Do NOT involve anyone outside of the marriage who cannot help the marriage to survive and eventually recover.

If your spouse won't go with you, then be the one to make the first step to seek professional help to strategize what can be done.

3. **Address your problems "in house" when it is best.**

In other words, don't work to stabilize your marriage at Aunt Sue's party or at a restaurant or any other location where others who shouldn't be involved can enter into and cause more harm. Take your problems into the privacy of your home or at a counselor's office (one who is **PRO**-marriage) — wherever you can get the best healing results. If you feel that some type of temporary separation is the only option that will get you through this crisis, then be careful in doing so. Above all, make sure that your "emergency mindset" is working toward *fixing* the marriage problems, rather than escaping them to find a dysfunctional coping mechanism which would further damage your relationship.

4. Don't bring other family members or friends in to "help" unless you BOTH agree outside help would be best.

It isn't productive to have others choosing "sides" — pitting you against each other. But also, be honest with yourselves as to whether your marriage can heal without additional help.

Sometimes it is better to lower your pride for a season and get the help of a few people, than it is to keep things private until a divorce forces matters out into the public.

5. Don't involve your children.

Children don't need to be involved when you are in "crisis mode." Marital issues can be harmful for them to see and listen to all of the gory details of what's going on. It just complicates that which you need to do to get your marriage stable again.

And even though this should go without saying, if someone outside of the family is complicating matters, stay away from them —especially during this time.

"Crises are capable of wounding us deeply, no matter what or who causes them. Some of the most destructive and devastating traumas are those caused or created by those we care about most: our family and friends.

An example of this type of hurt could be a marriage in which an affair has occurred. The emotional and social pressure on the wounded partner is far-reaching and undoubtedly long-term. There is nothing that causes more emotional pain in a marriage than to be betrayed by someone you love, depend on and trust" *(Mitch Temple, from Focus on the Family article, "Is Your Marriage in Crisis?").*

6. **If there is an affair partner or a "friend" involved that a spouse feels threatened by, cut all ties.**

The fact of the matter is that you cannot divide your romantic "affections" with someone other than your spouse and expect your love to remain or build back up again.

If it is a "friend" who is causing problems, then it would be helpful to ask yourself the question, "Is this person really my friend?" "Friends" do not attempt to divide you as a married couple.

7. **If a family member is causing problems, the spouse who is related to him or her should diplomatically ask the family member to back away.**

This way, both of you can better work on stabilizing your marriage. And then you can eventually see what is to be done in the future —if this family member safely to re-enter your lives in a way that is not divisive.

"I am convinced that the emotional scars and wounds that occur in families are some of the most unpleasant and damaging on the face of the earth. Crisis is difficult in and of itself, and even more so when it is caused by people whom we care for" *(Mitch Temple, from Focus on the Family article, "Is Your Marriage in Crisis?").*

Keep in mind what Jesus said about the marriage relationship: "They are no longer two, but one.

Therefore what God has joined together, let man not separate." *(Matthew 19:6)* Not letting man (or woman) separate you in your marriage, includes friends or family members, or even yourself, to shove your spouse out of his or her rightful place in your heart and priorities.

This is a time for you and your spouse to concentrate on your relationship and NOT to involve those who don't contribute to the healing process.

8. Be intentional about your words. Don't be "reckless" with your tongue.

This is a time to open the lines of communication, not slam each other's ears and attitudes shut.

That means no name-calling, slander, belittling, yelling, screaming, or using the "silent treatment" to try to get your point across. Those are antics that immature children employ to get their way. We're given some great advice in the Bible to challenge this type of behavior: "When I was a child, I talked like a child, I thought like a child, I reasoned like a child. When I became a man (woman), I put childish ways behind me" *(1 Corinthians 13:11)*.

"If you're stuck in a pattern of put-downs and cruelty, consider its destructive effects: It tears down your mate's confidence. It puts you both in a negative light around others. Also, it blocks intimacy, and erodes your spiritual well-being. In addition, it teaches your children to be inconsiderate and unkind. "Fortunately, you don't have to remain locked in this dance of disrespect. You can take productive steps to freedom, and changing your patterns can affect your children and your children's

children!" *(Louis McBurney, from article, "When Couples are Cruel")*

9. Stop doing that which is causing more damage.

"Agree to stop the conflict. Yes, agreeing to stop the conflict can be that simple. Agree that you will not fight about anything, and will set hot issues aside until you've learned the skills necessary to talk about them in a respectful way. Agree to end defensiveness, so you can truly listen to the needs and concerns of your mate" *(From a question and answer article written by Dr. David Hawkins, please read,* Help! We Love the Lord, But We're Cruel to Each Other*).*

10. Make the agreement: "We will do whatever is needed to stabilize this marriage."

It can be called, "Cocooning." "Crisis takes our breath away, sometimes completely knocking us off our feet. An unexpected death. Sudden illness. Natural catastrophe or family emergency. A good name ruined. Financial disaster. Critical times stir up anguish, fear, or anger so fierce it can destroy a marriage. If we turn inward, withdrawing from our spouse, we risk damaging the beautiful oneness of marriage.

"So how do couples respond to crisis? What helps? I believe God wants us to cocoon together, as husband and wife. Doing so strengthens a relationship, eases heartache and deepens love for each other through the shared pain" *(Karilee Hayden).*

If one of you steps over the line during this time of cocooning and is "reckless" in word or deed, give each other the permission to give some type of (polite or humorous) signal or say a certain phrase (that isn't offensive, which you both agree upon) to signal the other to stop. The other spouse is *not* to take offense at this, but rather stop. This is a time to start re-training yourselves to do things differently and change offensive words and behavior both now and in the future.

You might think this will seem unnatural and awkward not to just blurt (or hurl) out whatever comes into your mind. And honestly, it will be, at least for a while. But as Dr. Phil McGraw asks, "How's it working for you the way you've been doing things so far?" The obvious answer is "Not too well" because if it *was* working for both of you, your marriage wouldn't be in crisis mode. (Remember that marriage is about partnership, not about being an "island of me.") Again, what you are trying to do is first, stabilize the marriage so more damage isn't being done, and then work on doing things in the future in healthy, rather than destructive ways.

One Issue at a Time

After you have put the above tools into place, work through issues, one at a time. If it takes several days (or more) to work through one issue, so be it. Try to be patient with the process. You didn't get to a crisis stage overnight and you won't fix it in that timing either.

You may be impatient. But remember that you promised each other that you would live together for the rest of your lives. Taking the time and making the effort NOW to work through your issues together is only a fraction of the time you promised each other. Be patient. "Perseverance must finish its work so that you may be mature and complete, not lacking anything" *(James 1:4)*.

As you work through your issues, you may find it very, very difficult at times. But that is all part of the process. Don't give up. "Let us not become weary in doing good, for at the proper time, we will reap a harvest if we do not give up" *(Galatians 6:9)*

Chapter 7

HAVE I MET EVERYONE?

The following is a question that can be most awkward when raised in any relationship. While you don't want to seem as though you do not trust your partner, left to chance, some things will only come up unless questions are asked. Therefore, the following questions may become the most important questions to ask in a developing relationship:

Family History/Origin:

- Do you know everyone in your family?
- How familiar are you with your family history?
- Are there health issues that you should be aware of ش s you continue throughout your relationship?
- Do you have any additional children?

    Typically, this question should be asked during the dating phase; however, it is intriguing how easily some information can be overlooked or simply not shared for many reasons.

Relationship History:

Other questions to ask might include the following:

- Do you have any unfinished business with other individuals?
- Are there relationships that have not ended completely?
- Do you share property and/or investments with anyone from past relationships?
- Are there any shared accounts that you may have forgotten about? How about that life insurance policy? Who is the beneficiary? When did you last review this information to ensure that everything is accurate?
- Do you have any relationships that have not been fully closed, such as blended relationships (co-parenting)?
- What are your feelings toward the other parent? Can we have peace in our home, or will a previous relationship cause a consistent issue for us because of your hatred for your child(ren)'s other parent or unresolved feelings toward one another?

These discussions should typically happen during the dating phase, yet they can be missed, and meeting everyone for the first time can really present a challenge.

Meeting the family and friends for the first time can be a welcoming or traumatic experience. Which of the two that prevails is up to you. A few questions you will need to ask yourself are:

- How have I presented this person to my family/friends?
- Is this person going to be a massive shock to everyone?
- Am I selfish in my view (it's my life and relationship)?

For the best possible outcomes and experiences of meeting each other's family and friends, it is extremely important that you have conversations before the in-person meeting. If you are aware that there are differences which need to be addressed, save your partner the stress by addressing those issues with your family/friends ahead of the in-person introductions.

The way in which we introduce relationships can often determine the success of the entire group relationship. It is useless for us to become so intentional about the current relationship that we often do not allow our family/friends to embrace and adequately welcome our partner into our family/friend circle.

Consider the introductions below.

*AGE DIFFERENCE (10 YEARS OR MORE)

We understand that people find love at different stages in their life. According to a study from Emory University, couples with only a one-year age difference in relationships have just a 3% chance of divorcing. Compare that study to these percentages:

- 18% chance of divorce for a 5-year age gap
- 39% for a 10-year age gap,
- 95% for a 20-year age gap.

According to MYDOMAINE.COM, after analyzing 3,000 couples, the researchers ultimately found that the more significant the age gap between the couples, the more likely the couples are to get a divorce. Yet, there is one caveat to this rule. Statistics show that couples who do manage to make it past the two-year mark, no matter the age gap, are approximately 43% less likely to split up. However, no matter how healthy the relationship is, the opinions of others can impact the couple, since there are so many questions that family or friends may ask when they notice a significant age difference. This, my friend, is not the time to be defensive, because you have already taken the first step, which was an introduction. The most important factor is that the relationship works for the two of you and that you have considered the most powerful challenges you could have in the future. Here are some other areas to consider when there may be a significant age difference:

- HEALTH & AGING: Make sure that you are prepared for the older spouse to lose some vitality. At some point, an aging spouse may need long-term health care and may no longer be able to do certain hobbies that you both enjoy.
- EXPECTATIONS: Expectations are essential for all couples, but an awareness of your partner's expectations is particularly important when you're both far apart in age.
- MUTUAL INTERESTS: Explore each other's worlds by trying new activities, meeting new people, and remaining involved in each other's lives.

INTERRACIAL & INTERCULTURAL PARTNERSHIPS

The world has changed greatly over the years. In 2012, interracial couples comprised of 17% of all married couples in the United States. It has changed so much that race is no longer something that we will allow to hinder our love relationship for the other person. While we are totally into one another, we clearly understand that everyone will not understand our relationship dynamic. You must be so convinced that this is the right relationship that you will defend it at all cost. This cost can include moving away from relationships that you may have had for years before this one. I read an article in Psychology Today that had a critical piece of advice for interracial couples:

"All couples benefit from social approval of their relationship, but this is arguably even more vital for partners in interracial relationships. They have to contend with social bias, a problem that monoracial couples don't have to face." In other words, your relationship is more vulnerable to haters and individuals that disagree with your relationship than different types of couples.

Next, be sure to present a united front. You should know where you both stand on race issues, and you should be ready to defend your position. To present a united front successfully, you must have meaningful conversations behind closed doors.

INTERCULTURAL PARTNERSHIPS

Intercultural relationships may be complicated to maintain. While they are very charming at first, and the differences are exciting and fun, over time, intercultural partnerships can become a challenge. In many instances, we have not taken the appropriate time to thoroughly research the culture of our partner. We have only gone by what they, their family, and friends have mentioned to us. Have you done your proper research? Are you willing to make the cultural differences and demands that may come with this partnership as time progresses? The same Psychology Today article that I mentioned above had three strong tips for intercultural relationships. I will share the tips and cite the article information at the end of the chapter so you can read the article in its entirety.

- Demonstrate awareness of a partner's culture, and actively make room for a partner's cultural beliefs, practices, and traditions.
- Find ways to express appreciation for a partner's culture, such as conveying admiration, learning their native language, or cooking traditional cultural dishes.
- Treat a partner's unique cultural background as an exciting opportunity for discovery. Take active steps to learn more about their cultures, such as reading about it or asking questions in the spirit of interest and curiosity.

You can read more here:

(https://www.psychologytoday.com/us/blog/your-future-self/201808/strengthening-interracial-relationships)

SAME-SEX PARTNERSHIPS

On June 26, 2015, the U.S. Supreme Court ruled by a count of 5-4 that same-sex marriage would be legal in all fifty states. Since that time, more same-sex couples have been able to legally recognize their relationships.

Define Your Relationship Early

It is essential to realize that everyone does not view the word "relationship" the same way. So the first step to a happy same-sex partnership is making sure that you and your partner define "relationship" in the same context. In a hook-up culture (regardless of sexual identity), you both must agree that "relationship" means "exclusive." Many couples experience a crisis at this embryonic stage of the relationship. It seems simple, but if you and your partner decide to be exclusive, take action to help this decision stick. Whatever you choose, make sure both of you agree, or resentment will build, and your relationship is unlikely to last. Finally, do everything you can to foster support for keeping your relationship intact, and do not venture virtually or physically into situations that tempt you to stray.

Be Clear About Your Sexual Roles

Ensure your partner knows if you prefer a dominant or submissive role within the sexual relationship. Few relationships are happy without enjoyable physical intimacy. Just know that voicing your preference is critical to help you not make the mistake of pretending you are something that you are not, or could never be, to attract this person you are interested in.

Develop Strong Emotional Intimacy

Relationships built primarily on a sexual connection typically will not last long-term. Strengthening your mutual emotional intimacy through daily check-ins and meaningful conversations will help you stay together through the inevitable conflicts that crop up in all relationships.

Establish Your Own Identity

When same-sex partners come together, like straight couples, it is natural to experience a sense of fusion, a state where you do everything together. It can be exciting to have finally found your "one." It is amazing to be with someone who "gets" you, and if you are not careful, you will want to spend every waking moment with your partner. However, I encourage you to maintain your separate outside interests and continue to work on self-development. All healthy relationships need breathing room to keep things interesting; yours is no exception. Please avoid the temptation to look to your partner to fulfill all your emotional and intellectual needs. This temptation often leads to trouble and the demise of even the best relationships.

Dealing with Your Past, Present, and Future

First, keep all past relationships in the past. Avoid the temptation to compare your current partner to your former one(s). If you are struggling with past relationships, get counseling, and heal from prior wounds to protect your current relationship.

Next, protect your future by realizing that most people have a past. If you decide to have an open/non-exclusive relationship for any reason, you need to discuss your health testing frequency and protection rules.

If you have decided that marriage is right for the both of you, research how you might legally protect your partner so that he or she has spousal rights such as power-of-attorney, medical benefits, or death benefits. These rules can vary from state to state, so make sure that you know your rights and protect one another legally.

Chapter 8

RELATIONSHIP FRUSTRATION

The older we become, the less flexible we are. While our waning dexterity may be difficult to admit, it is a very true statement. The one exception is in the case of sickness or tragic accidents that may leave one vulnerable to change without choice. Other than that exception, a tenured partnership/marriage can consider separation due to the lack of communication. This happens often to empty nesters. When people have lived busy lives for most of their relationship, and their lives slow down, they discover how much they have grown apart—events like children heading off to college, retirement, career change (freeing up time), and not being forced to spend extended amounts of time together. If people are not careful, this can very well become their plight. They can become "fed up," argumentative, irritable to the point of wanted to become legally separated. Here are some ways that you can avoid this unfortunate situation:

OPTIONS

Options are the way of life as the world continues to change. Both partners must understand that each has freedom of choice. A toxic relationship can go undiscovered for a reasonable amount of time before either party realizes the toxicity. I have sat with many couples who had fallen into very toxic relationships but had allowed sex and many other extracurricular activities to be what they would turn to as opposed to communicating their way through the unwitting changes at hand. Also, I have consistently seen domestic violence result from toxic relationships.

Additionally, I see mental abuse, and at times, a consistently negative outlook develop after long periods within a toxic relationship. This negativity will cause one of the partners to ask themselves, "Can I do this for the rest of my life?" In the early stages of my relationship counseling and mentorship, I would encourage partners to "stick it out" while assisting them in navigating through different paths of mental abuse and negativity. The unfortunate part of these situations was that no matter how much we practiced those exercises, the underlying issue of the relationship's being toxic would not allow them to progress.

My colleague and friend, Rainah Davis wrote a book entitled *Break Up or Make Up*, and she shared some ways that both partners can identify and avoid the toxicity in their relationship. Please allow me to share those with you.

1. The arguments are getting worse— (you used to argue rarely or occasionally, but now you have verbal disagreements regularly or almost daily).

    If regular communication results in disagreement, arguments, and/or insults, then negativity will flood into your relationship. Often, couples who land here frequently started here to a lesser degree. You and your partner may never have communicated well, and the arguments intensified after engagement or marriage. Unfortunately, this type of relationship decline is common with mismatched or incompatible couples. However, these symptoms of incompatibility foretell the delayed but inevitable death of an unhealthy relationship. When I say "unhealthy," I mean several points:

A. Unequally matched— which means that you want different things. For example, materialistically, one person wants to live in a mansion for parties, guests, and extended family. The other person wants a lovely townhome with just enough space for the occupants. Or you want different paths in life: one person wants the couple on a "career and business path," and the other wants to pursue, primarily, a "family path"—where the family is first, and career is second.

This divergence is going to cause a vast divide that eventually will lead to severe issues. Keep in mind that nothing is wrong with either objective; the problem arises when the couple lacks agreement on which path they should take collectively.

B. The relationship was rushed, and the individuals never really got to know one another. Often, some couples end up together because physical attraction and sexual activities are high on their list of priorities. At the same time, the consideration of emotional bonding is not as high on or even on the list. These couples can survive a long time off of passion, physical attraction, and physical chemistry. Those attributes alone; however, are usually not enough to keep couples together for a significant amount of time. Nor do they typically result in a holistically healthy relationship.

C. The individuals in the couple do not like anyone else in their significant other's inner circle (this can extend to family, friends, or colleagues). If no one in the husband's family likes his wife's family (parents, siblings, cousins, etc.), that dislike will likely lead to an uphill battle waiting to be fought. If the wife doesn't like any of her husband's former classmates, teammates, or fraternity brothers, some counselors would suggest that you might not really like him. There are instances where people are friends with people who are opposites of themselves, but that mix is rare. Most of the time, you are friends based on the similarities, and the differences make the friendship more fun.

D. If you do like the members of your significant other's circle, but those individuals cause issues for your relationship, these issues can also cause difficulties. One of the most significant challenges for couples is trying to remain close to people whose lives may be very different from theirs once they go from being single to married or from being an individual to being in a serious, committed relationship. For example, if you are married, but all your friends are single, they may not understand why you need to go home by a particular time, or they may not understand why you have to go home at all, depending on their values and what your crew's "norm" is.

If you and your cousins have always gone clubbing and afterwards go to your favorite eating spot, stay late, and you typically make it home sometime around sunrise, your prospective spouse may not be okay with that. This instance is especially true if your partner was unaware of this ritual before you became committed to one another or got married. Also, know that even if the individuals all like each other, if the external relationships negatively impact you and your significant other's relationship over an extended period, then the relationship could become significantly damaged.

2. You are "speaking at one another," but not "communicating" with each other.

    "Speaking" may mean that while you may not be arguing, the communication is strained, negative, or apathetic. Examples of this scenario can be frequent sarcasm, feeling that one or more of the parties is not listening, or negative body language. Additional examples can be disrespectful behavior (such as rolling eyes, sucking teeth, walking out while the person is still talking, calling the other person out of his or her name, embarrassing him or her in front of others, and incessant nagging). Keep in mind that it is entirely possible to speak to someone every day with no love, no care, or without any real intimacy. If every interaction has become more of a neutral-feeling transaction than a loving or at least positive exchange, the relationship is in a bad state. You know that you are reaching this point when you begin to feel that you are "on the outside looking in" to his or her life or if you begin to feel more like roommates than lovers/spouses.

3. The (seemingly) smallest things cause WWIII to break out between the two of you.
    A. You can hardly agree on anything
    B. Activities you used to enjoy with each other, you no longer enjoy.
    C. When you try to remember what started the fight, you can rarely recall it because the smallest things repeatedly set off major explosive arguments.
4. Counseling does not help.
    A. One or both of you refuse to go to counseling—or the worse outcome—
    B. Counseling seems to make your situation worse.

        If you agree to go to counseling, and counseling doesn't positively affect your relationship, this outcome is usually a serious red flag. Here are a few suggestions to potentially achieve an effective result:

        - Make sure that you seek counsel from a qualified, non-biased third-party.

Please Note:
   A. I worked for non-profit and religious organization settings for over twenty years, and unfortunately, not all clergy are skilled at counseling people who are experiencing marital difficulty.
   B. Qualified counselors will tell you when your case is beyond their expertise. I do not recommend that you go to counseling for years without having breakthroughs.

If you are experiencing any of the above issues in your relationship, you will need to reset your relationship in order to get back on the right track. If you do not, other pieces of your relationship will begin to unravel.

The older you get, the less likely you are able to keep up "the show." "The show" is what I describe as public joy that masks private misery. This misery comes from no longer being attracted to your partner physically, mentally, or sexually. "The show" also masks the unfulfillment caused by the "seasons of change." "Seasons of change" mark instances such as

- my interest has changed; my partner has not.
- my partner/our life together is repetitive and boring.
- we no longer have common interest/we have grown apart.

If you do not address these instances, your relationship will be reduced from intimate life partnership to mere roommates.

危机

Chapter 9

BEDROOM GUESTS

I am not writing either to condemn or to encourage your bedroom activity since I believe that this matter is extremely private and a decision that should be agreed upon by both partners. Instead, this discussion is about types of sex: porn, sex toys, additional partners, etc. The primary considerations are consent and agreement.

Consider: If you have *any* reservations about sex toys, wait until you and your spouse can discuss this act. Your spouse should never force you to do something that feels wrong. And you shouldn't give in to such pressure, as that type of coercion would violate your own integrity.

I stumbled upon an article from Focus on Family that reminds us that the Bible says three important things about the meaning and purpose of marital sex — principles that inform and shape all physical intimacy expressions in marriage:

- It's central to a husband and wife becoming *one flesh* (Genesis 2:24).
- It's how they participate in the ongoing work of God's creation through the pleasure and delight of procreation (Genesis 1:28).

- It's intended to serve as a symbol of the union between Christ and His Church (Ephesians 5:31-32).

We live in a time where people are more "open" in bedroom practices than ever before. Additionally, I am aware that pornography, sex toys, and including additional parties during your time of intimacy could potentially harm what is intended to be precious, intimate, and special in your relationship.

Again, the goal is not to judge your decisions but rather to provoke thought about an area which involves many ramifications. Know that your spouse may agree to something because he or she loves you. Believe it or not, your partner may be very uncomfortable with the idea of bedroom guests in any form, but because of your passion behind it, he or she allows it. In cases like this, it will only last for a certain amount of time.

The idea that "guests" are needed for intimate moments could suggest that one is not satisfied with his or her partner exclusively. While many could disagree with this statement, I believe that a couple's partner alone should be enough. A couple should want his or her, partner, to feel special, exclusive, and attractive as he or she is more than enough unless the couple agrees that the bedroom guests make it feel that way.

But I caution you If **either individual the relationship has a history of pornography use, sex addiction, or sexual abuse, the couple should definitely steer clear of using sex toys altogether.** Using them will reinforce a predisposition to depersonalize sexual intimacy with his or her spouse, which might encourage involvement in dark, pornographically-related sexual practices. Be sure that you both have honest conversations and agree on what will happen sexually, going forward.

Whatever you do sexually, make sure that you are doing it together.

> **1 Corinthians 7:5 "Do not deprive one another, except perhaps by agreement for a limited time, that you may devote yourselves to prayer; but then come together again, so that Satan may not tempt you because of your lack of self-control."**

Sometimes, couples argue, and then they use sex as a form of punishment or "getting even" with their partner, but this punishment is clearly sin. It is not their call to make. When a spouse withholds sex as a result of a disagreement, that spouse may make it more tempting for their mate to seek a relationship with someone else. This is something that should never occur! It's just a good practice to end each day positively, such as seriously contemplating extramarital sex.

Make sure that you have agreement, love one another, and grow together.

危机

Chapter 10

PARTNER POLITICAL VIEWS

You would be surprised to know how many partnerships are divided politically. According to a 2016 survey, 17% of Republicans and Democrats who are married or living with their partner said that their spouse or partner belonged to a different political party. And lately, opinions across party lines are particularly tense.

Does this political division mean that one is right, and the other is wrong? The idea that one political preference is right and the other is wrong is absolutely not the case. In many relationships, this idea is assumed rather than discussed. I take time to mention political differences in this book because these differences can become a major crisis in your relationship when your views are different and not communicated… or communicated and strongly disagreed with.

It is absolutely acceptable to have a different view and opinion politically. I believe that it is both mature and respectful to share with one another and ensure that you both understand what makes up each other's political stance. Additionally, it is important to note that political perspectives can change over time. Your views may alter, and this shift will require additional conversation. Just think about it:

- What happened when your partner decided to get involved politically?
- Were you ready for this?
- Have you had this discussion?
- Do you have a complete understanding of why? Do you understand the passion?

Here are some things that you can do to ensure that political differences do not derail your relationship's peace and unity:

1. Acknowledge each other's opinions/views, and respect them.

   While you don't have to agree with your partner's opinion, it's essential to recognize his or her point of view and willingness to share it with you.

2. Be determined not to take your partner's opinion and views personally.

   Sometimes there will be issues so crucial that couples may never agree on them, and assure your partner that their disagreeing with you is acceptable. Allowing space in your relationship to respectfully disagree should be expected because agreeing on everything is unrealistic. Never forget that freedom of speech is one of the foundations that make America so unique! Embrace your differences, and refuse to allow your feelings to get hurt.

3. Cite facts, not opinions.

   Experts advise focusing on how you discuss your differences rather than focusing on the opinions themselves. When you reach a peak during a heated political debate, that peak is the optimal time to bridge your differences by agreeing to disagree.

Greens. Neocons. Ultraliberals. Remember that Americans are a diverse group of parties. Republicans, Democrats, and Libertarians hold very different views. These different points of view can cause political discussions which are challenging but hopefully occur in a civilized manner. Even if you and your mate have agreed to disagree, arguments can come out of nowhere when the conversation topic turns to an upcoming election.

Finally, understand that backgrounds, economic position, race, religion, and experiences all play a part in formulating our political beliefs. The more committed you are to understanding "why" your partner has formed the views he or she has, the less affected your relationship will be by political views.

危机

Bonus Chapter 11
AVOID O.P.P.

Now, I am about to date myself. The rap group, Naughty by Nature, released O.P.P., a hit in late summer of 1991. According to Wikipedia, "O.P.P." is a song by the American rap group Naughty by Nature. It was released on August 24, 1991, as the lead single from their self-titled debut album "Naughty by Nature." The song was one of the first rap songs to become a pop hit when it reached No. 6 on the Billboard Hot 100 and No. 35 on the U.K. Singles Chart. Its declaration, "Down Wit' O.P.P.," was a popular catchphrase in the U.S. in the early-1990s. The song was written by Larry Mizell, Larry Mizell, Fonce Mizell, Freddie Perren, Deke Richards, Berry Gordy, Kay Gee & Treach.

Just in case you have forgotten the lyrics, or never have heard the song, I have taken the liberty to share a portion of the words below — just enough to give you the idea about what the song is about.

> O.P.P., how can I explain it
> I'll take you frame by frame it
> To have why' all jumpin' shall we singin' it
> O is for Other, P is for People scratchin' temple

The last P…well… that's not that simple
It's sorta like another way to call a cat a kitten
It's five little letters that are missin' here
You get on occasion at the other party
As a game 'n it seems I gotta start to explainin'
Bust it
You ever had a girl and met her on a nice hello
You get her name and number and then you feelin' real mellow
You get home, wait a day, she's what you want to know about
Then you call up, and it's her girlfriend or her cousin's house
It's not a front, F to the are to the O to the N to the T
It's just her boyfriend's at her house (Boy, that's what is scary)
It's O.P.P., time other people's what you get it
There's no room for relationship there's just room to hit it
How many brothers out there know just what I'm gettin' at
Who thinks it's wrong "cause I'm splittin' and co-hittin' at
Well if you do, that's O.P.P., and you're not down with it
 But if you don't, here's your membership
[Chorus]
You down with O.P.P. (Yeah you know me) [Repeat]
Who's down with O.P.P. (Every last homie)
You down with O.P.P. (Yeah you know me) [Repeat]
Who's down with O.P.P. (All the homies)

O.P.P. means "other people's "property." The "property" refers more explicitly to the sexual body parts of the individual.

The recent relationship admission of a celebrity's "entanglement" is an example. Although separated at the time of the initial encounter, once the celebrities reconciled, the third party was then entangled with "O.P.P." The celebrity's description of "entanglement" was humorous for many, but in truth, most accurate.

Free Dictionary

1. *To cause to become twisted together or caught in a snarl or entwining mass:*
2. *To involve in a complicated situation or in circumstances from which it is difficult to disengage:*

Collins Dictionary

A complicated or difficult relationship or situation.

Cambridge Dictionary

A situation or relationship that you are involved in and that is difficult to escape from

Merriam Webster Dictionary

The act of being wrapped or twist together

Involvement in a perplexing or troublesome situation

So as you can see from the definitions above, the celebrity seemingly chose the perfect word to describe her relationship with this young man (twenty years her junior). Before we talk about how you can avoid your entanglements, I want to explain the components of an entanglement a little further.

Relationship expert Kim Von Nerg describes *entanglements* as having one or more of these characteristics:

1) **One or both are emotionally immature. This often is accompanied by some destructive behaviors in one's individual life.**
2) **The romance repeats dysfunctional patterns such as:**
    (a) communication breakdowns
    (b) over-emphasis on sex (overtime)
    (c) angry outbursts followed by distancing
    (d) emotionally shutting down
    (e) one or both tend to feel victimized by the other
    (f) withholding the truth
    (g) an obsessive need to stay connected motivated by a fear of abandonment
    (h) one of both are not able to set boundaries
3) **Withholding parts of you for fear of driving the other person away**
4) **Predominant sense of unsafety**
5) **A lot of conflict and power struggles**
6) **Often feeling not seen or understood**
7) **More negative feelings than positive about the relationship**

In a sense, this is an unhealthy relationship. My goal is to make sure you and your partner are thriving in the healthiest relationship possible. One way to thrive is to focus on the two of you and your needs. One of the most significant factors leading to affairs and entanglements with O.P.P. result in "unmet needs." If you find a need going unmet long enough, you may venture out or fall into a situation with a person who meets that need.

If you are not healed from sexual abuse or suffer from a form of sexual addiction, it may not matter whether your relational needs are met or not because your "greed" or appetite for sex may rule you and cause you to find yourself in unsavory situations.

Recently, I had an opportunity to talk to a reformed womanizer. I mean, this guy had an epic run on his college campus. He was known as a ladies' man. His friends, frat brothers, and family were stunned when he settled down with a young lady and was entirely faithful to her.

At first, his family and friends assumed that there was something exceptional about his wife that "tamed" him from his exploits. However, upon further investigation, I learned that there were three components to his faithfulness.

1. He made a decision that he was ready to settle down and not hurt his mate. To each one of you reading, just know that you cannot make anyone faithful. The first step to "faithfulness" is being with someone who wants to be monogamous and committed to you and only you. There was no magical pill. The guy decided that he did not want to lie, hide his phone, or be on edge every time his phone rang. He decided he did not want to have to remember his lies and keep track of where he had told his wife where he was. He no longer wished to juggle multiple women. He was tired; actually, he said being unfaithful makes for an exhausting life after the thrill wears off, and frankly, he did not want to live that way any longer. Second, he

did not want to hurt his future wife, which meant he had to give up the other women before he got married to build up the skill of *"faithfulness."*

2. He was overly aware of his surroundings and environment. He told me that he quickly ejects himself from any place where he could get into trouble. This decision made perfect sense. All affairs, relationships, and entanglements start with glances that turn into conversations and conversations that lead to physical encounters.

3. He relied on self-control as a last resort. Sometimes you just have to be able to say politely or aggressively, "No, thank you; I am not interested." He pointed out that he did not say that he was married because some people like being involved with married people. Or that declaration opens the door for someone to ask you if you are *happily* married, and even if you are, there may be a day when you are not happy with your significant other. He always makes it a point to quickly shut the conversation down and then remove himself from the environment.

I was impressed and thought those are some great tips for staying out of trouble. Understanding the different types of entanglements and affairs will also help you avoid them.

Dave Carder, an affair authority, authored the books Torn Asunder: Recovering from Extramarital Affairs (1992) and Anatomy of An Affair: How Affairs, Attractions, and Addictions Develop and How to Guard Your Marriage Against Them, shares some profound perspectives regarding extramarital affairs.

Carder lists five types of extramarital affairs.

Class One: One-Night Stand - An unplanned affair that happens between strangers, typically occurs as a result of a stimulant such as alcohol and takes place in secret.

Class Two: Entangled Affair - An affair that develops gradually. Sexual intimacy typically happens over a long period, after a friendship is established. This affair develops as the result of an emotional deficit lacking in the primary relationship.

Class Three: Sexual Addiction - This behavior is a never-ending, unsatisfied need for compulsive sexual encounters. It is typically the result of an inappropriate sexual contact that occurred in childhood or adolescence.

Class Four: Add-On Affair - This affair directly answers a specific unmet need. Typically, the primary relationship is a happy one, but a necessary yet vital need is unfulfilled. Dr. Willard Harley Jr.'s book, *His Needs Her Needs: Building an Affair Proof Marriage* lists the top five emotional needs for women and men as:

HER Top 5 Emotional Needs (on average):
1. **Affection**
2. **Conversation**
3. **Honesty & Openness**
4. **Financial Support**
5. **Family Commitment**

HIS Top 5 Emotional Needs (on average):
1. Sexual Fulfillment
2. Recreational Companionship
3. Attractiveness of Spouse
4. Domestic Support
5. Admiration

When any of these needs are left unmet it creates a longing that can be fulfilled by someone outside of the marriage.

Class Five: Reconnection - This is a tricky case. Carder explains that this affair starts as rekindling of a "first love" or "old flame." Social media has made it easier than ever to reconnect to lost love. Carder says, "Time creates a nostalgia that intensifies infatuation." These relationships cause you to feel as if you married the wrong person, and the fantasy life you imagined with the old connection seems larger than life. These feelings can be difficult to fight through, and unfortunately, by the time you realize the feelings were just a fantasy, there can be irreparable harm to the primary relationship.

I wanted to take some time to share this information so that you can be vigilant against any outside relationship that damages your marriage. As the old adage says, "An ounce of prevention is worth a pound of cure." You must be determined to safeguard your relationship.

TIPS FOR AFFAIR RECOVERY

1. **Accept your part in the affair.** It is often more common to hold the unfaithful person accountable for his or her actions than dealing with the cause of the affair. However, if you have contributed to your spouse's affair through neglect, abuse, or abandonment, I urge you to deal with all the aspects of the causes.
2. **Decide whether you can forgive the adulterer.** A relationship will not recover without forgiveness. If you are a person who holds grudges and are unwilling to practice what my pastor describes as "intimate forgiveness," your relationship is doomed, quite frankly. *Intimate forgiveness* is a decision to love someone despite their transgression while holding them accountable for real repentance. No amount of counseling can fix a relationship in which the offended party refuses to let the affliction go. The counseling just will not work. The offender often is trying hard to fight the urge to return to the affair, and if he or she feels as though his or her relationship at home is hopeless, he or she will relapse.
3. **Decide if you really want to stop cheating.** If you are too far gone in your extramarital affair to completely cut it off, you should leave your marriage. There is nothing worse than watching a forgiving spouse being reinjured over and over again by an unrepentant or undisciplined individual. Please love your spouse enough to let them go if you are not going to stop hurting them through your actions.
4. **Get qualified counselors.** Please seek help from a professional who is not associated with either of you.

You need an unbiased individual who is skilled in martial counseling to help you get through this rough patch.

Finally, if you or your spouse are/is recovering from an entanglement or affair, just know that you can survive it and move past it, but you both have to commit to each other and the process.

I wish the best for you both,

Tyrus

www.ingramcontent.com/pod-product-compliance
Lightning Source LLC
Chambersburg PA
CBHW070430010526
44118CB00014B/1981